Unterrichtsmodell

Series Editor: Hans Kröger

Poetry

by Angela Luz

EINFACH ENGLISCH

Best.-Nr. 041227 4

Schöningh

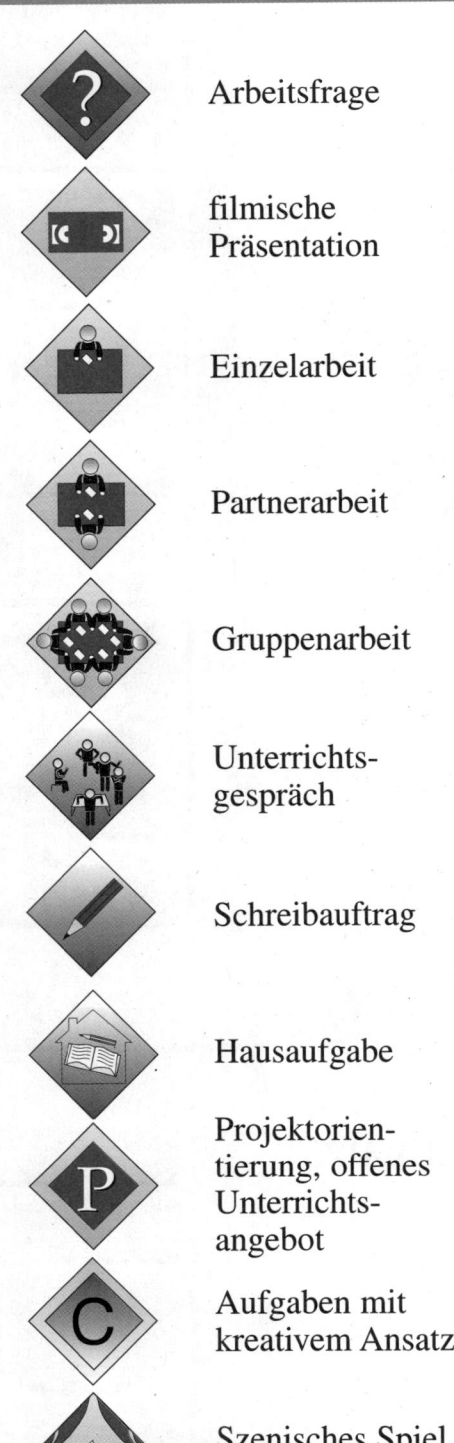

Arbeitsfrage

filmische Präsentation

Einzelarbeit

Partnerarbeit

Gruppenarbeit

Unterrichts-gespräch

Schreibauftrag

Hausaufgabe

Projektorien-tierung, offenes Unterrichts-angebot

Aufgaben mit kreativem Ansatz

Szenisches Spiel, Rollenspiel

Website
www.schoeningh.de
E-Mail
info@schoeningh.de

Vorwort

Der Titel der Reihe **EinFach Englisch** ist Ziel und Programm zugleich. Einerseits sollen Schülerinnen und Schülern literarische Zusammenhänge erklärt und ihnen damit der Zugang zu klassischen, aber auch neueren literarischen Werken erleichtert werden, und dies soll auf sprachlich einfache Art und Weise erfolgen, wodurch man der heutigen Schülergeneration sicherlich eher gerecht werden kann als mit schwierigen und komplexen Ansätzen. Andererseits sollen Lehrkräften erprobte und aus der Praxis stammende Unterrichtsmodelle angeboten werden, die ihnen einen raschen Zugriff auf unterschiedliche Materialien ermöglichen und einen Leitfaden für die Behandlung fiktionaler Texte oder die Analyse von Filmen im Unterricht bieten. Die Modelle können direkt und ohne Umschweife eingesetzt werden, langes Einlesen und eine zeitintensive Beschäftigung mit dem Stoff sind nicht erforderlich, wodurch die Arbeit, insbesondere die Unterrichtsvorbereitung von Lehrerinnen und Lehrern, erheblich erleichtert werden kann.

Schnell erhält man einen Überblick über **Figurenkonstellation** und **Inhalt** und kann sich problemlos entscheiden, ob ein Werk für eine bestimmte Reihe geeignet ist. Man weiß vorab, welche **Klausur** mit welchen Schwerpunkten geschrieben werden kann, und kann dieses bei der konkreten Planung eines Kursabschnittes entsprechend berücksichtigen. **Arbeitsblätter** sind als Kopiervorlagen gestaltet und **Tafelbilder** sind eingebettet in die **Leitfragen** zum eigentlichen Unterrichtsgeschehen, d. h., Material, das eingesetzt werden soll, befindet sich dort, wo es gebraucht wird; langes Suchen entfällt. **Piktogramme** geben optische Hilfen und Hinweise, sodass leicht zu erkennen ist, welche **Sozial-** bzw. **Arbeitsformen** sich bei den jeweiligen Aufgaben anbieten.

Die Unterrichtsmodelle basieren auf bewährten Verfahren der Textinterpretation und der Filmanalyse, dabei fließen neuere Erkenntnisse und Ansätze zu einer modernen Textrezeption angemessen ein. Der Umfang des Materials ist auf die tatsächlichen Gegebenheiten der Unterrichtspraxis abgestimmt und es sollte möglich sein, das Unterrichtsmodell vollständig und nicht nur in Auszügen im Rahmen einer Unterrichtsreihe einzusetzen. Das Prinzip der „**Components**" ermöglicht es darüber hinaus den Benutzern, unterschiedliche Reihen zu konzipieren, die an unterschiedlichen thematischen Schwerpunkten oder methodischen Fertigkeiten orientiert sind und ganz den individuellen oder kursspezifischen Bedürfnissen angepasst werden können. Dabei erheben die Unterrichtsmodelle nicht den Anspruch der Vollständigkeit, sondern eher den der Machbarkeit und Praxisnähe.

Sprachliche Betreuung: Thomas van Breda;
Illustration S. 3: Susanne Kuhlendahl/Verlagsarchiv Schöningh

© 2002 Schöningh Verlag
im Westermann Schulbuchverlag GmbH
Jühenplatz 1–3, D-33098 Paderborn

Druck: WB-Druck, Rieden am Forggensee

Druck   5   4   3   2   Jahr   06   05   04   03

ISBN 3-14-041227-4

Alle deutschsprachigen Teile dieses Werkes folgen der reformierten Rechtschreibung und Zeichensetzung.

Components

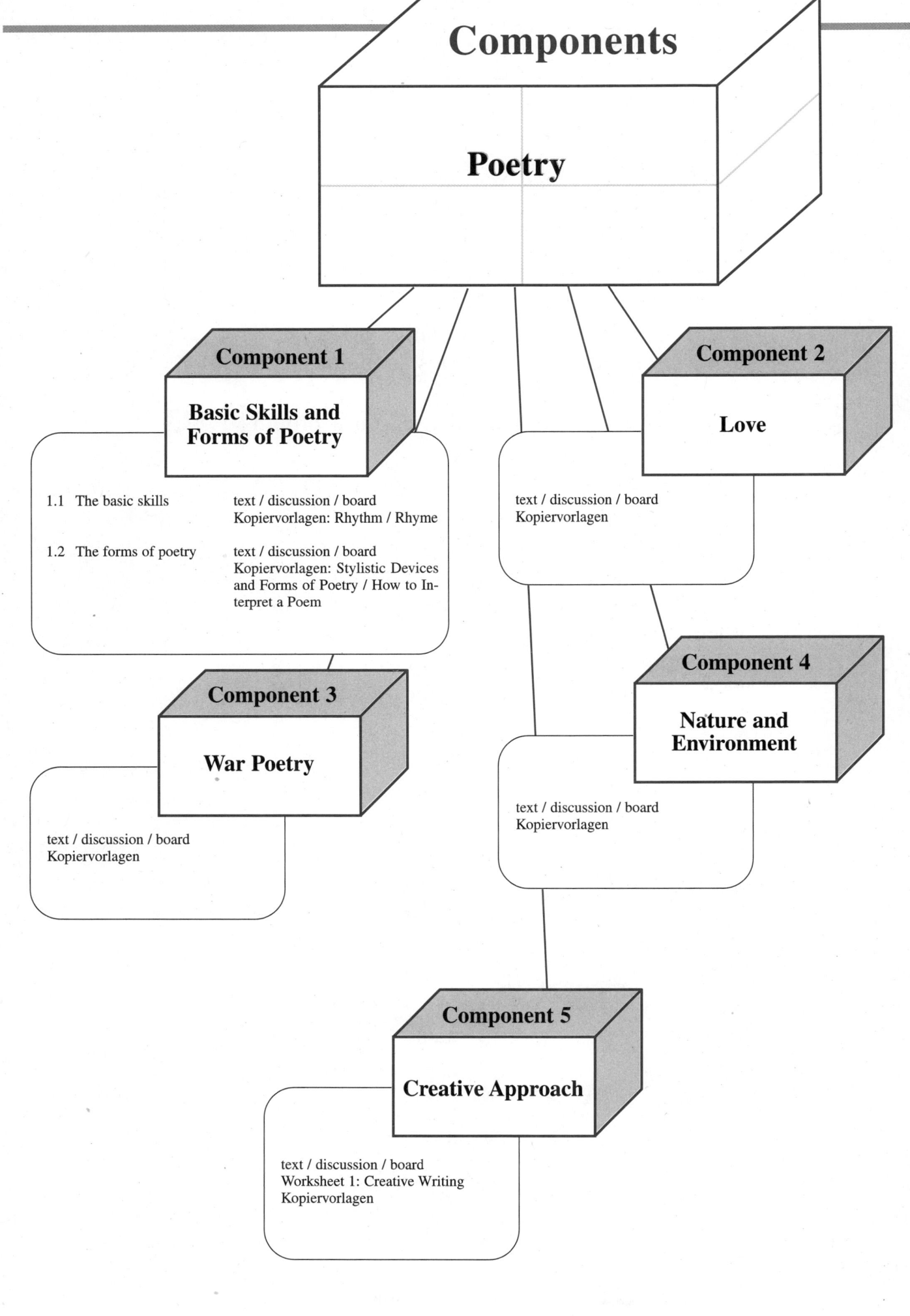

Poetry

Component 1

Basic Skills and Forms of Poetry

1.1 The basic skills   text / discussion / board
Kopiervorlagen: Rhythm / Rhyme

1.2 The forms of poetry   text / discussion / board
Kopiervorlagen: Stylistic Devices
and Forms of Poetry / How to Interpret a Poem

Component 2

Love

text / discussion / board
Kopiervorlagen

Component 3

War Poetry

text / discussion / board
Kopiervorlagen

Component 4

Nature and Environment

text / discussion / board
Kopiervorlagen

Component 5

Creative Approach

text / discussion / board
Worksheet 1: Creative Writing
Kopiervorlagen

Pat Ingoldsby, *Open Season*

"Run for your lives," shrieked the poems. "Here
come the students!"
They sprang from their books and panicked
around the library.
Students chased after them with marker-pens,
explanatory texts, study notes, test questions
and murderous intent.
One terrified poem hanged itself in a broom
cupboard.
Two more went down a plughole in the
washroom.
"Don't let them get away," yelled the teacher.
"They'll warn the others!"
With relentless certainty they cornered one
poem behind the radiator.
They stunned it with a tranquilliser dart.
"Now!" said the teacher. "Find out what the
poet really meant."

Contents

The Authors

Im vorliegenden Unterrichtsmodell kommen Dichterinnen und Dichter aus verschiedenen Jahrhunderten und Herkunftsländern zu Wort. Im Folgenden werden in alphabetischer Reihenfolge die wichtigsten im Unterrichtsmodell vertretenen Autorinnen und Autoren kurz vorgestellt.

Asquith, Herbert (1852–1928)

Herbert Asquith was the 1st Earl of Oxford and Asquith. He was a British Liberal politician who was prime minister from 1908 to 1916.

Auden, W(ystan). H(ugh). (1907–1973)

Born in York, Auden achieved early fame in the 1930s as a hero of the left during the Great Depression. In 1939, he settled in the US and became a US citizen. Auden was not only a poet but also a playwright who collaborated with Christopher Isherwood. In 1936 he married Thomas Mann's daughter Erika. In 1948 Auden won the Pulitzer Prize.

Blake, William (1757–1827)

William Blake was an English poet, artist, engraver and visionary. He was one of the most important figures of English Romanticism (style of art, music and literature that was common in Europe in the late 18th and early 19th century which describes the beauty of nature and which emphasizes the importance of human emotions). Blake illustrated the two most important volumes of his lyrical work *Songs of Innocence* (1789) and *Songs of Experience* (1794) himself.
Blake frequently saw angels and had other visions which influenced his work.

Brooke, Rupert (1887–1915)

Brooke was a talented youth who died during World War I. Before the war he studied in Germany and travelled in Italy. He spent a year (1913/14) in the USA, Canada and the South Seas.

Ewart, Gavin (1916–1995)

Gavin Ewart was a British poet of light verse.

Heaney, Seamus (born 1939)

Heaney was born and raised in Northern Ireland and has always explored in his poetry the violent roots of the conflict in his homeland. He was educated at Queen's University in Belfast where he later worked as a lecturer. Since 1989 he has been Professor of Poetry at Oxford. In 1995 he was awarded the Novel Prize for Literature.

Henri, Adrian (born 1932)

Adrian Henri studied fine arts at King's College, Newcastle. He is one of the trio of Mersey Poets (poets from Liverpool near the river Mersey – often writing about down-to-earth topics in a witty style. The other two are Roger McGough and Brian Patten). He is also a painter and a musician.

Keats, John (1795–1821)

John Keats was an English Romantic poet who was born in London. He had a great talent for drawing on classical mythology and medieval lore for his works (traditional knowledge and stories about a subject), as demonstrated in his odes. He started to study medicine but soon abandoned science for poetry. Suffering from tuberculosis he travelled to Rome in 1820 hoping to be cured there. However, he died there in the following year.

Lawrence, D. H. (1885–1930)

D. H. Lawrence was an English writer whose most famous novels are *Sons and Lovers* (1913) and *Lady Chatterley's Lover* (1928). He also wrote short stories and poems, e. g. *Birds, Beasts and Flowers* (1923) and *Collected Poems* (1928).
Because of his wife's German nationality and his own disapproval of World War I the Lawrences were turned out of their home in Cornwall in 1917. From then on they travelled and rarely spent time in England.
Lawrence suffered from tuberculosis and died near Nice, France.

Marvell, Andrew (1621–1678)

Andrew Marvell was an English poet who is considered one of the best secular Metaphysical poets. (Metaphysical poets belong to a school of poetry which began at the end of the 16th century and developed in the 17th century. They wrote like philosophers and dealt with metaphysical and thus difficult questions. Their poems are clever riddles that the educated reader has to solve.)
He supported Oliver Cromwell and tutored Cromwell's ward from 1653–1657. In 1657 he became assistant to John Milton as Latin secretary in the foreign office.

McGough, Roger (born 1937)

Like Adrian Henri, he is one of the so-called Liverpudlian Mersey Poets. He is famous for his witty style.

Milton, John (1608–1674)

John Milton is regarded as one of the best English writers after Shakespeare. His *Paradise Lost* is ranked as the greatest epic poem in the English language. Milton wrote poetry in English and Latin. From 1638–1639 he travelled with a servant to Italy and visited Florence, Rome and Naples.

Owen, Wilfred (1893–1918)

Owen enlisted in 1915 in the Artists' Rifles. The experience of trench warfare influenced his work considerably. In June 1917 he was invalided out of the army and returned home where he met Siegfried Sassoon who was impressed by his work.

Owen returned to France in August 1918 where he was killed a week before Armistice Day.

Sandburg, Carl (1878–1967)

Carl Sandburg was an American poet, historian and novelist. His most famous poem *Chicago* published in 1920 was received favourably at the time.

His popular biography of Abraham Lincoln (1926 and 1939) won him the Pulitzer Prize in history in 1940.

Sassoon, Siegfried (1886–1967)

Siegfried Sassoon was an English poet and novelist. He became famous for his antiwar poetry.

Sassoon enlisted in World War I and was wounded twice in France. He became a friend of Wilfred Owen whose work he published after Owen was killed at the front.

Shakespeare, William (1558–1616)

William Shakespeare lived during the reign of two monarchs, Elizabeth I and James I. He was born in Stratford-on-Avon. He married Anne Hathaway when he was 18 and had three children with her. The early years of his life are obscure, but by 1592 he was a well-known actor and playwright in London. From 1594 till 1611 he was a member of a group of players called the King's Men. They built the Globe Theatre and became London's most famous theatre group. He retired in 1611 in Stratford with his family and died there five years later.

Walcott, Derek (born 1930)

Walcott was born in the West Indies, he is of mixed Afro-Carribean and white race which is often reflected in his poetry. In 1992 he was awarded the Nobel Prize for Literature.

Wilde, Oscar (1854–1900)

Oscar Wilde was an Irish wit, poet and dramatist. In 1884 Wilde, a self-professed dandy (a man at the beginning of the 20th century who dressed in expensive, fashionable clothes and was very interested in his own appearance), married Constance Lloyd and had two children with her. Because of his homosexuality he was prosecuted in 1891 and sentenced to prison in 1895. Disappointed with society he died in a hotel room in Paris. His most famous play is *The Importance of Being Earnest*. His aphorisms (aphorism: a short, cleverly phrased saying which is intended to express a general truth) are still frequently quoted.

Williams, William Carlos (1883–1963)

William Carlos Williams was an American poet who succeeded in making the ordinary appear extraordinary through the clarity of his imagery. He was a poet and medical doctor.

Williams also wrote novels and short stories. In 1965 he was posthumously awarded the Pulitzer Prize for poetry for his 1962 *Pictures from Brueghel and other poems*.

Wordsworth, William (1770–1850)

William Wordsworth was a major Romantic poet. His *Lyrical Ballads* (1798) written with S. T. Coleridge helped launch the English Romantic movement. Being orphaned early he and his brothers were sent to a grammar school at Hawkshead.

In 1797 he was reunited with his sister Dorothy with whom he lived together for the rest of his life.

Klausuren

Im Folgenden finden sich drei Klausurenvorschläge, die man nach der Bearbeitung des ersten oder des jeweils thematisch passenden *Component* einsetzen kann.

Klausur Nr. 1 eignet sich für einen Leistungskurs, da der zugrunde liegende Text eine recht eigenständige Bearbeitung erfordert. Die Frage nach der Struktur des Gedichtes verlangt ein relativ hohes Maß an Textverständnis; auch gibt es wenige der gängigen Stilmittel wie Anaphern, Alliterationen u. Ä. zu entdecken, sondern es müssen Satzstrukturen und komplexe Gedankengänge untersucht werden. Thematisch schließt diese Klausur an die Texte aus *Component 3: War* an.

Klausur Nr. 2 bezieht sich inhaltlich auf *Component 4: Nature and Environment*. Das Gedicht von Seamus Heaney führt den Leser zurück in die Kindheit des Dichters, der seine Begegnung mit Fröschen beschreibt. Da dieses Gedicht mehrere ungewöhnliche Vokabeln enthält, erfordert es eine gründliche Erarbeitung, die vermutlich nur von Leistungskursschülern geleistet werden kann. Auch ist der Transfer vom beschriebenen Treffen mit den Fröschen zu der Erkenntnis, dass der Sprecher von der Welt der Kinder in die der Erwachsenen tritt, also eine Initiationssituation beschrieben wird, nicht leicht zu leisten.

Dagegen eignet sich Klausur Nr. 3 sehr gut für die Bearbeitung in einem Grundkurs. Thematisch passt dieser Text zu *Component 2: Love*. In ähnlicher Weise wie W. H. Auden in *Victor* beschreibt Derek Walcott in seinem Gedicht *A Country Club Romance* den Lebensweg einer Person im Zeitraffer. In diesem Fall geht es um eine junge Frau, die einen Schwarzen heiratet. Die Schülerinnen und Schüler können die Problematik dieser Verbindung leicht erkennen und sind daher in der Lage, dieses Gedicht zu interpretieren.

Bei allen Klausuren empfiehlt es sich, die Texte zu Beginn der Bearbeitungszeit einmal laut vorzutragen.

Notizen:

_____

_____

_____

_____

_____

_____

_____

_____

_____

Peter Porter, *Your Attention Please*

The Polar DEW has just warned that
A nuclear rocket strike of
At least one thousand megatons
Has been launched by the enemy
5 Directly at our major cities.
This announcement will take
Two and a quarter minutes to make,
You therefore have a further
Eight and a quarter minutes
10 To comply with the shelter
Requirements published in the Civil
Defence Code – section Atomic Attack.
A specially shortened Mass
Will be broadcast at the end
15 Of this announcement –
Protestant and Jewish services
Will begin simultaneously -
Select your wavelength immediately
According to instructions
20 In the Defence Code. Do not
Take well-loved pets (including birds)
Into your shelter – they will consume
Fresh air. Leave the old and bed-
ridden, you can do nothing for them.
25 Remember to press the sealing
Switch when everyone is in
The shelter. Set the radiation
Aerial, turn on the geiger barometer.
Turn off your Television now.
30 Turn off your radio immediately
The Services end. At the same time
Secure explosion plugs in the ears
Of each member of your family. Take
Down your plasma flasks. Give your children
35 The pills marked one and two
In the C. D. green container, then put
Them to bed. Do not break
The inside airlock seals until
The radiation All Clear shows
40 (Watch for the cuckoo in your

to comply to act according to an order or request

aerial antenna

© Schöningh Verlag, Best.-Nr. 041227-4

perspex panel), or your District

Touring Doctor rings your bell.

If before this, your air becomes

Exhausted or if any of your family

45 Is critically injured, administer

The capsules marked "Valley Forge"

(Red pocket in No. Survival Kit)

For painless death. (Catholics

Will have been instructed by their priests

50 What to do in this eventuality.)

This announcement is ending. Our President

Has already given order for

Massive retaliation – it will be

Decisive. Some of us may die.

55 Remember, statistically

It is not likely to be you.

All flags are flying fully dressed

On Government buildings – the sun is shining.

Death is the least we have to fear.

60 We are all in the hands of God,

Whatever happens happens by His Will.

Now go quickly to your shelters.

perspex strong transparent plastic used instead of glass

retaliation hurting s.o. because they have hurt you

Assignments

1. In this poem the people of a country are advised to follow certain instructions. What situation is the country in? What is the advice like?

2. Explain the structure of the poem. Take into consideration the speaker's intention.

3. Comment on possible reactions of people listening to this announcement.

4. Write a farewell letter of one of victims.
   OR
   Imagine you are one of the survivors of this nuclear attack. Tell your children about this day.

© Schöningh Verlag, Best.-Nr. 041227-4

perspex strong transparent plastic used instead of glass

Erwartungshorizont zu Klausur 1

zu 1: Peter Porter's poem *Your Attention Please* is an announcement made shortly after a nuclear attack on a country. The speaker is obviously a radio broadcaster who is giving the government's orders to the public or even a government official who is giving orders to the public about how to behave in this emergency. There has been a nuclear attack on major cities of the speaker's country by an enemy whose identity remains unclear. The enemy has launched several missiles carrying nuclear bombs and only $10^{1/2}$ minutes remain for the attacked country's inhabitants to react. It seems that there have been threats of such an attack since everybody owns a copy of the Defence Code (l. 20), obviously a manual about how to behave in case of a nuclear attack. The advice that is given:
- select the correct wavelength (l. 18)
- leave pets behind (ll. 20/21)
- leave old and sick people behind (ll. 23/24)
- press sealing switch in shelter (ll. 25/26)
- turn on geiger barometer (l. 28)
- turn off TV and radio (ll. 29–31)
- check ear plugs of family members (ll. 31–33)
- give pills to children, put them to bed (ll. 34–37)
- in emergency use red pills (ll. 43–48)
- do not despair (l. 59)
- go quickly to the shelters (l. 62)

zu 2: The poem starts with the description of the situation after the enemy's attack. The first part (ll. 1–20) consists of three long sentences. It informs the listener about the attack, the $10^{1/2}$ minutes remaining till the impact of the bombs and about possible religious consolation given in a short mass or service.

Then a lot of commands follow. The first two commands are structured as a parallelism: command – explanation: Do not take ..., they will ... . Leave ..., you can do ... (ll. 21–24). Then there are nine short orders (till l. 37) giving instructions. The anaphora "turn on ... turn off ..., turn off ..." (ll. 28–30) underlines the urgency of the message.

In the next part of the poem there is again a long explanation which ends rather abruptly when the listeners are instructed to offer certain pills to injured members of their family for painless death (l. 48). While the pills used to put children to sleep are kept in a green box (l. 36), green symbolising hope, the pills for painless death are found in red containers (l. 47), red symbolising danger.

The announcement ends with the rather worthless information that the President, called "our President" (l. 51), as "our cities" in line 5, creating a sense of common fate, has taken steps to retaliate. Lines 57–58 want to set an optimistic mood with the use of the patriotic symbol of the flags, stressed by an alliteration "flags are flying fully" (l. 57) and the cliché that "the sun is shining" (l. 58).

The statement "Death is the least we have to fear" (l. 59) can only be seen as a paradoxical statement under these circumstances. At the end of the poem the fatalistic statement "Whatever happens happens by God's will" (l. 61) stressed by the chiastic structure is refuted by the final command to hurry to the shelters. The speaker's intention is to inform the population of a rather dangerous and urgent situation combined with the wish to prevent people from panicking.

zu 3: Although people seem to have been well-prepared for an attack like the one taking place here, it seems inevitable that mass hysteria will take over and a major mass panic will occur.

Students' answers may vary from cool reception, since there has been some kind of warning of the possibility of such an attack, to the confession that they would panic too, because the nuclear threat is still one of mankind's worst nightmares.

zu 4: Again, the answers will vary depending on the students' view of the situation. A letter, however, should express a lot of anxiety and fear. Whether hope of survival is expressed or a depressed state of mind is reflected depends entirely on the student. The same is true for the answer to the second possibility of this creative task. The narration could resemble the telling of an adventurous time or rather reflect the panic and fear of the people involved.

Notizen:

_____

_____

_____

_____

_____

_____

_____

_____

_____

_____

_____

_____

_____

_____

_____

_____

_____

_____

Seamus Heaney, *Death of a Naturalist*

All year the flax-dam festered in the heart
Of the townland; green and heavy headed
Flax had rotted there, weighted down by huge sods.
Daily it sweltered in the punishing sun.
5 Bubbles gargled delicately, bluebottles
Wove a strong gauze of sound around the smell.
There were dragon-flies, spotted butterflies,
But best of all was the warm thick slobber
Of frogspawn that grew like clotted water
10 In the shade of the banks. Here, every spring
I would fill jampotfuls of the jellied
Specks to range on window-sills at home,
On shelves at school, and wait and watch until
The fattening dots burst into nimble-
15 Swimming tadpoles. Miss Walls would tell us how
The daddy frog was called a bullfrog
And how he croaked and how the mammy frog
Laid hundreds of little eggs and this was
Frogspawn. You could tell the weather by frogs too
20 For they were yellow in the sun and brown
In rain.

Then one hot day when fields were rank
With cowdung in the grass the angry frogs
Invaded the flax-dam; I ducked through hedges
25 To a coarse croaking that I had not heard
Before. The air was thick with a bass chorus.
Right down the dam gross-bellied frogs were cocked
On sods; their loose necks pulsed like sails. Some hopped:
The slap and plop were obscene threats. Some sat
30 Poised like mud grenades, their blunt heads farting.
I sickened, turned and ran. The great slime kings
Were gathered there for vengeance and I knew
That if I dipped my hand the spawn would clutch it.

sods matted roots of grass
sweltered to suffer from oppressive heat
bluebottles big blue flies

slobber saliva dribbling from the mouth
frogspawn mass of eggs produced by frogs

tadpoles aquatic larva of frogs

rank stinking

cocked to stand or stick up conspicuously

poised to balance evenly
blunt rounded

vengeance revenge

Assignments

1. This poem is divided into two parts. Explain the division.

2. The atmosphere in this poem changes. Describe the change, taking into account the stylistic devices used by the poet.

3. Give an interpretation of the poem's title.

4. Comment on the thesis that children growing up in cities miss many opportunities of developing naturally.
   OR
   Write a dialogue between the speaker and his mother after what has happened.

© Schöningh Verlag, Best.-Nr. 041227-4

Erwartungshorizont zu Klausur 2

zu 1: In his poem *Death of a Naturalist* Seamus Heaney describes a piece of land in the middle of his hometown. There is a place where flax grows and rots in the sun. A lot of insects are attracted by the process of decay. Frogs also live in that area and so frogspawn can be found and collected there. The speaker of this poem is a young boy who loves collecting frogspawn. He brings it home and even takes it to school where his teacher explains to the class everything there is to know about frogs. One day, however, he encounters the frogs while they are copulating and suddenly he is frightened by them and does not dare to take any of the frogspawn.

zu 2: In the first part of the poem Seamus Heaney describes a young boy who is fascinated by frogspawn and its development into tadpoles and eventually into frogs. You can see that he is still quite young when he says "But best of all ..." (l. 8), which evokes the image of a young child describing exciting things. His description of his teacher talking about "daddy frog" (l. 16) and "mammy frog" (l. 17) shows that he is probably still in primary school. As an interesting afterthought he adds that frogs can predict the weather (ll. 19–21). Again, this is something typical of a young child. In addition to these stylistic devices there are many enjambements in this poem, e.g. ll. 8–10 or ll. 10–15. These enjambements strengthen the impression that an excited child is talking. In the second part of the poem his attitude towards the frogs changes. He is no longer fascinated by them, but on seeing them copulate he becomes suddenly very frightened of them. The frogs are no longer harmless daddy frogs and mammy frogs, but they are "gross-bellied" (l. 27) and the sounds they make when moving are "obscene threats" (l. 29). He compares them to "mud grenades" (l. 30) and calls them "great slime kings" (l. 31). The alliteration in line 25 "coarse croaking" emphasizes the atmosphere of danger and fear. The speaker's panic becomes clear in the enumeration in line 31 "I sickened, turned and ran".

zu 3: The title of the poem implies that somebody died. However, when reading the poem you realize that not a person has died, but that something has died in a person, namely the innocent love of watching frogs and collecting something from nature. The speaker of the poem used to be a child naively playing around in nature. One day he becomes aware of the fact that nature is not harmless but can also be threatening. The fact that the frogs are copulating appears to scare him because he does not yet understand what these animals are doing. Nevertheless, his innocence is lost. In that sense a naturalist has died.

zu 4: The comment about where children grow up more naturally could include a comparison between what children can experience in the countryside and what opportunities there are for them in a city. A conclusion should be supported by several reasons. The dialogue should include the boy's excitement, his breathlessness and his curiosity and lack of understanding of what he has seen.

Derek Walcott, *A Country Club Romance*

The summer slams the tropic sun
Around all year, and Miss Gautier
Made, as her many friends had done,
Of tennis, her deuxième-métier.

5 Her breathess bosom rose
As proud as Dunlop balls;
She smelled of the fresh rose
On which the white dew falls.

Laburnum-bright her hair,
10 Her eyes were blue as ponds,
Her thighs, so tanned and bare,
Sounder than Government bonds.

She'd drive to the Country Club
For a set, a drink and a tan;
15 She smoked, but swore never to stub
Herself out on any young man.

The club was as carefree as Paris,
its lawns Arcadian;
Until at one tournament, Harris
20 Met her, a black Barbadian.

He worked in the Civil Service,
She had this job at the Bank;
When she praised his forearm swerve, his
Brain went completely blank.

25 O love has its revenges,
Love whom man has devised;
They married and lay down like Slazengers
Together. She was ostracized.

Yet she bore her husband a fine set
30 Of doubles, twins. And her thanks
Went up to her God that
Her children would not work in banks.

She took an occasional whisky;
Mr Harris could not understand.
35 He said, "Since you so damn frisky,
Answer this backhand!"

Next she took pills for sleeping,
And murmered lost names in the night;
She could not hear him weeping:
40 "Be Jeez, it serve us right."

deuxième-métier favourite pastime

laburnum *Goldregen*

bonds *Wertpapiere*

tournament meeting for contests
Barbadian someone from Barbados

swerve act of turning aside

to devise to plan
Slazenger manufacturer of balls, here: synonym for tennis ball
to ostracize to exclude by general consent from society, friendship, privileges

frisky lively, playful

Jeez Jesus

Her fleet life ended anno
domini 1947.
From Barclay's D. C. & O.
Her soul ascends to heaven.

45 To Anglo Catholic prayers
Heaven will be pervious,
Now may Archdeacon Mayers
Send her a powerful service.

Now every afternoon
50 When tennis soothes our hates,
Mr Harris and his sons,
Drive past the C. C. gates.

While the almonds yellow the beaches,
And the breezes pleat the lake,
55 And the blondes pray God to "teach us
To profit from her mistake".

fleet swift, rapid

Barclay's D. C. & O.
well-known British bank

pervious open, accessible
Archdeacon rank lower than
bishop

Assignments

1. Summarize in your own words the story of Miss Gautier's life.
2. Why is Mrs Harris ostracized? What effect does this have on her?
3. Walcott uses puns, metaphors and similes based on the game of tennis. List these references to the sport. What is their function?
4. Comment on the last two lines of the poem taking into account that this poem was written in 1952.
5. Walcott was influenced by W. H. Auden and his suburban ballads as for instance *Victor*. Can you trace this influence in *A Country Club Romance*?

© Schöningh Verlag, Best.-Nr. 041227-4

Erwartungshorizont zu Klausur 3

zu 1: Miss Gautier is a young white woman who works at a bank. Her hobby is playing tennis. One day, while participating in a tournament at her country club she meets Mr Harris, a black man from Barbados. She falls in love with him and marries him. From then on she is no longer accepted by her friends and family. She has twin sons and starts to drink and take sleeping pills. She dies in 1947, leaving her husband and sons behind, who are not allowed to join the country club. She is regarded as a bad example by other white young women.

zu 2: Mrs Harris is ostracized by society because she has married a black man. She is obviously not happy about that because she starts drinking whisky and taking pills. She dies quite young.

zu 3: The students here could list:
- summer slams (l. 1)
- tennis, her deuxième-métier (l. 4)
- Dunlop balls (l. 6)
- a set, a drink and a tan (l. 14)
- praised his forearm swerve (l. 23)
- Slazengers (l. 27)
- a fine set of doubles (ll. 29/30)
- answer this backhand (l. 36)
- when tennis soothes our hates (l. 50)

The references to tennis are used to satirize white colonial society at the beginning of the 20th century. The lifestyle of affluent white people who are only concerned about their entertainment and looks is criticized.

zu 4: Having suffered from her friends' and family's intolerance towards her husband Mrs Harris has become a bad example for other young white girls who hope that they will not fall in love with a black man and lose all the friendship they ever had. Students can go on to speculate on the importance of the time when this poem was written. They could be of the opinion that today Mrs Harris would not be treated as in the 1940s or that today's ostracization would look different.

zu 5: Students can name:
- story of a life told in a few stanzas
- everyday language
- direct speech
- heroine is not someone special, but an ordinary person
- reader feels sympathy for heroine

Notizen:

_____

_____

_____

_____

Konzeption des Unterrichtsmodells

In diesem Unterrichtsmodell findet sich eine Sammlung von Gedichten, deren Bearbeitung die Schülerinnen und Schüler dazu anregen soll, sich der Textsorte Lyrik ohne Scheu zu nähern und sich mit Freude mit diesen für sie ungewohnten Texten zu beschäftigen.

Als auflockernder Beginn der Unterrichtsreihe kann eine Kopie des Gedichtes der Einstiegsseite dienen, das auf lustige Art vor den Gefahren des Überinterpretierens warnt. Es empfiehlt sich, dieses Gedicht zu lesen und mit den Schülerinnen und Schülern kurz zu besprechen, dass Gedichte im Unterricht zwar gedeutet, aber dennoch auch mit Genuss gelesen werden sollten.

Die Gedichte wurden ausgewählt, weil sie bestimmte gedichttypische Merkmale aufweisen oder einen der Themenbereiche (Liebe, Krieg, Natur) besonders gut repräsentieren. Dabei bestimmen natürlich der Geschmack und die Leseerfahrungen der Verfasserin dieses Unterrichtsmodells die Auswahl ebenso wie die Intention, sowohl Klassiker des Genres als auch weniger bekannte Werke vorzustellen. Dabei sollten auch verschiedene Epochen und Herkunftsländer der Autoren berücksichtigt werden.

Eine kurze biografische Erläuterung zu den Autoren, sofern man diese recherchieren konnte, findet sich unter der Überschrift *„The Authors"*. Diese Angaben können entweder von der Lehrerin bzw. vom Lehrer vorgetragen oder als Einstieg für Schülerreferate genutzt werden.

Die Reihenfolge der Bearbeitung der einzelnen *Components* ist nicht zwingend vorgeschrieben; allerdings empfiehlt es sich, zuerst *Component* 1 zu bearbeiten, da dort eine Einführung in die wichtigsten Grundlagen der Mittel zur Gedichtinterpretation stattfindet. Je nach Interessenlage des Kurses können die Ideen und kreativen Ansätze, die im *Component* 5 vorgestellt werden, auch zwischen einzelnen thematischen Blöcken bearbeitet werden. Wichtig ist es, die selbst verfassten Texte nicht einzufordern, sondern die Schülerinnen und Schüler selbst entscheiden zu lassen, ob sie ihre Texte vortragen wollen. Wenn es dagegen keine Einwände gibt, sollten die Texte in der Klasse oder der Schülerzeitung veröffentlicht werden.

In **Component** 1 werden *rhythm, rhyme* und *language of poetry* anhand von so unterschiedlichen Gedichten wie beispielsweise Zulfiker Ghoses *Geography Lesson* und *Life Sculpture* von George Washington Doane erläutert. Im Anschluss an den ersten Teil dieses *Component* findet sich je eine Kopiervorlage zu den Themen *Rhythm* und *Rhyme*. Im zweiten Teil geht es um die Formen der Dichtung. Hier dient John Keats *Ode to a Grecian Urn* der Einführung der für Schülerinnen und Schüler schwierigen Form der Ode. Darüber hinaus werden Sonette (Shakespeare und Milton) vorgestellt. Abschließend sollen Gedichte von William Carlos Williams und D. H. Lawrence in die Form des *free verse* einführen. Im Anschluss an diesen Teil des *Component* finden sich Kopiervorlagen zu den Themen *Stylistic devices* und *How to interpret a poem*. Nach dieser Einführung kann man nach eigenem Geschmack aus den Themenvorschlägen Gedichtreihen zusammenstellen. Dabei können sowohl die Wünsche der Schülerinnen und Schüler als auch die zur Verfügung stehende Zeit die Auswahl bestimmen bzw. beeinflussen.

In *Component* 2 werden unterschiedliche Gedichte zum Themenkomplex Liebe präsentiert. Als Einstieg dient ein Gedicht aus dem 17. Jahrhundert von Andrew Marvell. Dieses Gedicht soll zeigen, dass auch im 17. Jahrhundert entstandene Liebesgedichte nicht notwendigerweise sentimental sind, sondern durchaus auch heute noch unterhaltsam sein können. Modernere Texte folgen, zum einen W. H. Audens Ballade *Victor,* zum anderen zwei kürzere Texte von Gavin Ewart und Rupert Brooke.

Component 3 stellt Gedichte zum Themenkomplex Krieg vor. Dabei kommen sowohl Dichter zu Wort, die ihre Erfahrungen im Ersten Weltkrieg in Dichtung umgesetzt haben (Asquith, Sassoon), als auch Dichter, die ihre Kindheitserinnerungen aus dem Zweiten Weltkrieg (Sheila Perry, Lois Clark) oder Erlebnisse aus anderen Kriegen in Gedichtform gebracht haben (Carl Sandburg).

In *Component* 4 werden Gedichte aus dem Bereich Natur und Umwelt vorgestellt. Dabei werden nicht nur Klassiker wie William Blakes *The Tiger* und William Wordworth's *The Daffodils* behandelt, sondern auch moderne Rezeptionen des zweitgenannten Werkes, zum einen eine feministische Deutung von Lynn Peters, zum anderen eine Vermischung dieses Gedichtes mit der Werbeanzeige eines Autoherstellers von Adrian Henri. Daneben findet sich hier ein Songtext von den Talking Heads.

In *Component* 5 werden die Schülerinnen und Schüler dazu angeregt, selbst Gedichte zu verfassen. Dabei sollen nicht nur feste Formen von Dichtung wie Limericks und Haikus, sondern auch freie Formen wie *Shape Poetry* vorgestellt und dann nachgeahmt werden.

Notizen:

_____

_____

_____

_____

_____

_____

_____

_____

_____

_____

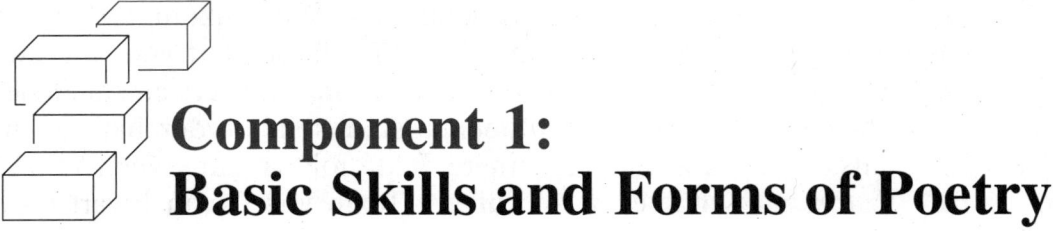

Component 1: Basic Skills and Forms of Poetry

1.1   The basic skills

Als Einstieg in das Thema *Poetry* könnte man folgende Vorgehensweise wählen: Man kann die Schülerinnen und Schüler fragen, was ihrer Meinung nach ein Gedicht zu einem Gedicht macht, bzw. was für Eigenschaften ein Gedicht haben muss. Je nach Leseerfahrung der Gruppe kann dieses *brainstorming* zu unterschiedlichen Resultaten führen. Eine Reihe von Begriffen wird sicherlich genannt werden.

What makes a poem a poem or rather what characteristics can you find in a poem?

rhythm	rhyme	stanzas	verses
poetic language	metaphors	imagery	meter / metre
	foot	romantic topic	

Im Anschluss an diese kleine Begriffsammlung sollten die Schülerinnen und Schüler ihre Vermutungen an einem Gedicht überprüfen können. Als Einstiegsgedicht bietet sich George Washington Doane's Gedicht *Life Sculpture* an, weil dieses Gedicht inhaltlich keine Schwierigkeiten bietet und man einige grundlegende Fachbegriffe wie metrisches Schema und Reimschema anhand dieses Textes gut erläutern kann.

Es bietet sich an, das Gedicht auf eine Folie zu kopieren und dann mit Hilfe von darüber gelegten Folien und bunten Folienschreibern die im Folgenden erarbeiteten Ergebnisse in der Klasse zu präsentieren.

Der Text wird verteilt und laut von einem Schüler / einer Schülerin vorgelesen. Falls man die Lerngruppe mit dieser Aufgabe nicht betrauen möchte, kann man auch selbst den Text vortragen.

Zunächst sollen die Zuhörer kurz zusammenfassen, wovon das Gedicht handelt.

What is this poem about?

This poem is about a young boy who sets out to carve a statue out of a marble block when he has an "angel-dream". His piece of work turns out to be exquisite. The author compares the boy's work with what we can achieve in our lives. When touched by God's command we may or will have the right dream (l. 4) or vision (l. 8).

George Washington Doane,
Life Sculpture

Chisel in hand stood a sculpture boy
With his marble block before him,
And his eyes lit up with a smile of joy,
As an angel-dream passed o'er him.

5 He carved the dream on that shapeless stone,
With many a sharp incision;
With heaven's own light the sculpture shone, -
He's caught that angel-vision.

Children of life are we, as we stand
10 With our lives uncarved before us,
Waiting the hour when, at God's command,
Our life-dream shall pass o'er us.

If we carve it then on yielding stone,
With many a sharp incision,
15 Its heavenly beauty shall be our own, -
Our lives, that angel-vision.

chisel wedgelike tool with a cutting edge at the end of the blade, often made of steel, used for cutting wood, stone, etc.

Solution

Chisel in hand stood a sculpture boy	U —|U —|U U —|U —
With his marble block before him,	U U —|U —|U —|U
And his eyes lit up with a smile of joy,	U U —|U —|U U —|U —
As an angel-dream passed o'er him.	U U —|U —|U —|U
5 He carved the dream on that shapeless stone,	U —|U —|U U —|U —
With many a sharp incision;	U —|U U —|U —|U
With heaven's own light the sculpture shone, –	U —|U U —|U —|U —
He's caught that angel-vision.	U —|U —|U —|U
Children of life are we, as we stand	U —|U —|U —|U U —
10 With our lives uncarved before us,	U U —|U —|U —|U
Waiting the hour when, at God's command,	— U|U —|U U —|U —
Our life-dream shall pass o'er us.	U —|U —|U —|U
If we carve it then on yielding stone,	U U —|U —|U —|U —
With many a sharp incision,	U —|U U —|U —|U
15 Its heavenly beauty shall be our own, –	U —|U U —|U —|U U —
Our lives, that angel-vision.	U —|U —|U —|U

Nach der inhaltlichen Zusammenfassung soll nun untersucht werden, weshalb dieser Text als Gedicht bezeichnet werden muss.

How do we know that this text is a poem?

- Rhyme scheme a, b, a, b
- Four stanzas with four verses (lines) each

Apart from the rhyme scheme are there other reasons why this is a poem?

- Rhythm in the language

How is this rhythm created?

- There is a rhythm because of the order of stressed and unstressed syllables.

Die Ergebnisse dieses Unterrichtsgespräches werden an der Tafel bzw. auf einer Overheadfolie festgehalten.

∪ — ∪ — ∪ ∪ — ∪ —
Chisel in hand stood a sculpture boy

The smallest unit of a meter is called a **foot.**
The most common foot in English poetry is the **iamb:**
∪ / meaning one unstressed syllable is followed by a stressed syllable.
Another common foot is the **anapest:**
∪∪ / meaning two unstressed syllables are followed by a stressed syllable.
Two less frequent feet are the dactyl (— ∪ ∪) and the trochee (— ∪)

Nach dieser Einführung in die Grundlagen der Metrik sollen die Schülerinnen und Schüler nun ihr erworbenes Wissen anwenden und eine metrische Analyse dieses Gedichtes durchführen. Dies kann in Partnerarbeit erfolgen. Die Ergebnisse können dann auf der Overheadfolie eingetragen werden (vgl. *Solution sheet).* Diese Aufgabe eignet sich auch gut als Hausaufgabe.

Analyse the metric pattern of this poem. Read the lines out loud and follow the natural pronunciation of the words.

Als Letztes bleibt die Benennung der Versmaße. Auch hier soll eine kurze Einführung genügen, damit der Inhalt des Gedichtes in den Mittelpunkt der Analyse rücken kann.

How many feet are there in one verse of *Life Sculpture?*

There are four feet per verse in this poem. In each stanza lines 2 and 4 end with an unstressed syllable (= feminine ending).

A meter consisting of four feet is called a tetrameter (Greek: tetra = four).
We also find pentameters (Greek: penta = five) in English verse.
We call *Life Sculpture* a poem written in iambic tetrameters because the predominant foot is the iamb.

Nach dieser formalen Analyse soll nun der Inhalt des Gedichtes näher untersucht werden.

Why does the author employ this rather complicated meter?

He uses a very simple rhyme scheme and so the meter can help to avoid monotony. The anapests give an extra liveliness to this poem that has a rather solemn content.

Nach der Beantwortung der letzten Frage steigt man am besten mit einer arbeitsgleichen Gruppenarbeit in die genauere sprachliche Untersuchung ein. Die Ergebnisse werden in einem Tafelbild festgehalten.

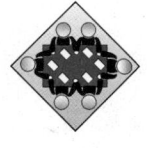

Now let us have a closer look at content and language of this poem. In this poem two things are compared. Let us collect key words that belong to these two groups. (Key word: a word that is important and essential for understanding and appreciating a text)

masonry	life
chisel	angel-dream
marble	angel-vision
stone	life-dream
sharp incision	heaven's light
sculpture	our lives

Whereas the first two stanzas refer to masonry and the young boy who wants to carve his marble block, the last two stanzas refer to life and what we can make of it. Thus there are many correspondences:

his marble block	our lives uncarved
an angel-dream	our life-dream
passed o'er him	pass o'er us
he carved the dream	if we carve it then
shapeless stone	yielding stone
with many a sharp incision	
heaven's own light	heavenly beauty
angel-vision	

The repetition of the identical line "with many a sharp incision" stresses the comparison.

Die sprachliche Ausformulierung dieses Vergleiches können die Schülerinnen und Schüler beispielsweise als Hausaufgabe leisten. Außer diesem Vergleich, der sich durch das ganze Gedicht zieht, kann man in diesem Text auch schöne Beispiele für Metaphern finden.

Explain the meaning of the metaphors employed in this poem.

One metaphor can be found in the third stanza, "lives uncarved", another one in the fourth stanza, "yielding stone". Both elaborate on the comparison that is predominant in this poem. Our lives are uncarved until we have a dream that gives us an idea of how to live our lives. Then we carve our lives and the "yielding stone", namely our inner life, is touched by an angel vision and will bring us fulfilment.

Das nächste Gedicht, das besprochen werden soll, heißt *Geography Lesson* und könnte als Friedensgedicht bezeichnet werden. Bevor der Text verteilt und von einem Mitglied der Lerngruppe laut vorgetragen wird, sollte die Frage gestellt werden, was die Schülerinnen und Schüler erwarten, wenn ein Gedicht diesen Titel hat. Nach dem Vortrag des Gedichtes steht die Frage nach dem Inhalt wiederum im Vordergrund.

Our next poem is called *Geography Lesson.* What do you think it is about?

- Poem about a teacher
- Some incident in a geography lesson
- Developing friendship in geography class
- Passing an exam

What is the poem really about?

The poem is not about school or teachers or students, but about why people fight each other. It is not a poem about school but a poem about peace. It describes what you see beneath you when flying over a city in an airplane. First you can see how the city developed and why it was planned the way it was. Then, flying even higher, you see not only one city, but several cities in their landscape, and so you understand why people settled where they settled. In the last stanza the plane has reached a height of six miles and from there it is no longer understandable why there are wars on earth.

Notizen:

_____

_____

_____

_____

_____

_____

_____

_____

_____

_____

Zulfiker Ghose, *Geography Lesson*

When the jet sprang into the sky,
it was clear why the city
had developed the way it had,
seeing it scaled six inches to the mile.
5 There seemed an inevitability
about what on ground had looked haphazard,
unplanned and without style
when the jet sprang into the sky.

When the jet reached ten thousand feet,
10 it was clear why the country
had cities where rivers ran
and why the valleys were populated.
The logic of geography –
that land and water attracted man –
15 was clearly delineated
when the jet reached ten thousand feet.

When the jet rose six miles high,
it was clear that the earth was round
and that it had more sea than land.
20 But it was difficult to understand
that the men on the earth found
causes to hate each other, to build
walls across cities, and to kill.
From that height, it was not clear why.

scale to decrease

haphazard not having an obvious plan

delineated to mark the edge of

Nach der kurzen Zusammenfassung des Gedichtes sollen nun die einzelnen Strophen genauer untersucht werden. Zuvor sollten jedoch in einem kurzen Lehrervortrag die Fachbegriffe *perfect rhyme, partial rhyme* und *enjambement* erläutert werden.

Look at the rhyme words "mile" (l. 4) and "style" (l. 7). Rhymes like those are called perfect rhymes because they have three characteristics:

---

perfect rhyme: mile / style

identically pronounced consonants:	l
identically pronounced vowels:	l / y
identical stress	

In contrast to this perfect rhyme there is a different one in lines 22 / 23: build / kill. These words only form a partial rhyme because the consonants are not identical (ld – ll) and the vowels are not pronounced quite identically.

Now let us have a look at lines 2 and 3 of the poem. In which way is there a difference to the lines in Doane's *Life Sculpture*?

In line 2 the sentence or sense unit does not end, but the sentence runs on. This is called a run-on line or an **enjambement.** The effect of this enjambement is to heighten the reader's attention and to prevent boredom due to too regular rhyme and metrical patterns.

Now let us analyse this poem.

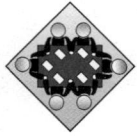

Nun können in einer arbeitsteiligen Gruppenarbeit die einzelnen Strophen des Gedichtes genauer untersucht werden. Jede Gruppe sollte eine Folie mit ihrer Strophe erhalten und diese mit Folienstiften beschriften, um im Anschluss an die Analyse die Ergebnisse der gesamten Lerngruppe präsentieren zu können. Diese Aufgabe eignet sich auch als Hausaufgabe, die Ergebnisse können zu Beginn der folgenden Stunde in Gruppenarbeit zusammenfassend auf die Folien eingetragen werden.

Analyse the structure of the poem. Look at rhyme scheme, meter and stylistic devices of your stanza. What does the author describe? In which way are form and content connected?

The poem consists of three stanzas of 8 lines.

Stanza 1:
rhyme scheme: a, b, c, d, b, c, d, a
metrical pattern: no regular pattern
There are two identical lines (ll. 1 + 8) which frame the stanza. The expression "when the jet sprang into the sky" (ll. 1 + 8) is surprising because you do not associate a jet with springing (moving quickly and suddenly towards a particular place).

The enjambements in lines 2/3 and 5/6 make the reading of the stanza difficult because the rhyming scheme is disturbed by them. However, the contrast between the apparently chaotic state of the city on earth and its obviously planned state when looked upon from the elevated viewpoint in a plane becomes clear in this stanza. The enjambements stress the reflective mood of the lines dealing with the surprising realization that there is a pattern behind chaos after all.

There is one line that starts and ends with "had" (l. 3) which stresses the development of the city. Also, the alliteration "<u>s</u>eeing it <u>s</u>caled <u>s</u>ix" (l. 4) and the contrast "inches to the mile" (l. 4) stress the planning behind the city's development.

Stanza 2:
rhyme scheme: a, b, c, d, b, c, d, a
metrical pattern: no regular pattern
The first and last lines of this stanza are identical so they embrace the stanza. The second line starts with the same words as the second lines of the first and third stanza: "it was clear". There is a decisive difference between "city" in the first stanza (l. 2) and "country" (l. 10) in the second stanza. Now not only one city can be seen, but also rivers and valleys. The "logic of geography" (l. 13) is that people settle along rivers and that valleys also attract settlers. There is one enjambement in lines 10/11 which stresses the contrast between the country and cities. The double reason for settlement named in the first half of the stanza (rivers, l. 11 and valleys, l. 12) is echoed in the second half by the contrasting phrase "land and water" (l. 14).

Stanza 3:
rhyme scheme: a, b, c, c, b, d, d, a
metrical pattern: no regular pattern
In the third stanza the first line is not repeated, but lines 17 and 24 rhyme. The adjective "high" in line 17 is echoed by the noun "height" in the last line of the poem. The rhyme scheme also differs from the first two stanzas. The reason for this difference is that in this stanza the topic is no longer just geography, but now the poem deals with the question why people find it necessary "to hate each other, to build / walls across cities and to kill" (ll. 22/23). This enumeration/climax/development from hating to killing stresses the uselessness of wars when looking at earth from such a remote viewpoint. Again there is the repetition of the contrast between water and land mentioned in stanza 2 in the expression "more sea than land" (l. 19).

Notizen:

_____

_____

_____

_____

_____

_____

_____

Rhythm

meter: pattern of stress in a poem

foot: smallest unit in a line as:

      iamb: ∪ — (abóve)

      trochee: — ∪ (ápple)

      anapest: ∪∪ — (unabrídged)
                this foot is used quite often in limericks

      dactyl: — ∪∪ (ténderly)

      spondee: — — (used very rarely, mostly to vary a iambic pattern)

caesura: pause in a verse indicated by // when scanning
                beauty is truth, truth beauty // – that is all (Keats Comp. 2)

to scan: to work out a poem's metrical pattern

monometer: one foot

dimeter: two feet

trimeter: a line consisting of three feet

tetrameter: a line consisting of four feet (Greek tetra = four)

pentameter: a line consisting of five feet (Greek penta = five)

hexameter: a line consisting of six feet, also called the Alexandrine

feminine ending: a line ending with an extra unstressed syllable

© Schöningh Verlag, Best.-Nr. 041227-4

Rhyme

stanza:	a group of lines of poetry forming a unit
complete rhyme:	for example: *bride – pride* or *rest – nest* A rhyme can be called a complete rhyme when there are / there is: 1. two identically pronounced consonants 2. two identically pronounced vowels 3. identical stress
partial rhyme:	one of the above mentioned criteria is not fulfilled for example: *hum – come* or *where – air* here the vowels are not pronounced identically
masculine rhyme:	a rhyme consisting of a single stressed syllable for example: *shine – mine*
feminine rhyme:	a rhyme consisting of two syllables: stressed – unstressed for example: *lighting – fighting*
end-rhyme:	a rhyme between two (or more) words at the ends of two (or more) lines
heroic couplet:	the last two lines of an Elizabethan sonnett
internal rhyme:	a rhyme between two words in the same line for example: Once upon a midnight *dreary,* while I pondered, weak and *weary* (Poe, *The Raven*)
eye-rhyme:	a rhyme that looks like a rhyme but does not rhyme, for example: And yonder all before us *lie* Deserts of vast *eternity*
continuous rhyme:	a rhyme scheme like aabbcc ...
alternate / cross rhyme:	abab cdcd
enclosing rhyme:	abba cddc
enjambement:	a run-on line, the sentence does not stop at the end of the line but goes on to the following line

Im Anschluss an die Bearbeitung dieses Gedichtes können den Schülerinnen und Schülern die Kopiervorlagen zu *Rhythm* und *Rhyme* verteilt werden, damit sie eine knappe Übersicht an der Hand haben, um Begriffe schnell nachschlagen zu können.

1.2   The forms of poetry

Im Rahmen dieses Unterrichtsmodells können nicht sämtliche Formen der Lyrik ausführlich besprochen werden. Es sollen daher nur einige Erscheinungsformen der Lyrik hier kurz vorgestellt und erläutert werden. Als Beispiele scheinen unerlässlich Ode, Sonett, Ballade und *Free Verse.*
Eine Ballade wird lediglich im Auszug vorgestellt (Oscar Wilde, *Ballad of Reading Goal)*, da diese Form der Dichtung hinreichend aus dem Deutschunterricht bekannt sein dürfte. Oden machen den Schülerinnen und Schülern erfahrungsgemäß Schwierigkeiten, da sie inhaltlich ernste Themen behandeln und in gehobener poetischer Diktion verfasst sind. Dennoch sollte auf ein Beispiel dieser Hochdichtung nicht verzichtet werden.
Wegen seiner Berühmtheit wurde John Keats *Ode on a Grecian Urn* gewählt. Wiederum wird eine Kopie des Gedichtes an den Kurs ausgeteilt. Bevor das Gedicht laut vorgetragen wird, sollte es wegen seiner ungewöhnlichen Sprache erst erarbeitet und verstanden werden. Zunächst sollte der Inhalt des Gedichtes geklärt werden. Bei leistungsstarken Lerngruppen kann die Erarbeitung des Inhalts des Gedichts auch als Hausaufgabe gestellt werden.

What is this poem about?

In "Ode to a Grecian Urn" John Keats describes a marble urn on which scenes from Ancient Greece are carved. He admires the eternal beauty of the nature scene and people.

What can you say about the vocabulary of this poem?

There are many forms of older English used in this poem. The narrator also employs words from a higher register than everyday English.

Wenn die Schülerinnen und Schüler diese Erkenntnis gewonnen haben, bietet sich eine Partnerarbeit an, in der das Vokabular genauer untersucht werden soll.

Identify the forms of older English that you can find in this poem.
Find words from a higher register of English and name their everyday English correspondences.

old forms:

thou (1)	=	you	art (40)	=	are
canst (3)	=	alte Form für can	dost (44)	=	does
		2. Ps. Sg. (vgl. kannst)	doth (45)	=	does
ye (12)	=	you	shalt (47)	=	shall
hast (19)	=	have (vgl. canst)	sayst (48)	=	say
wilt (20)	=	will			

higher register:

sylvan (3)	=	rustic	sensual ear (13)	=	real ear
deities (6)	=	gods	bliss (19)	=	happiness
mortals (6)	=	people	bid adieu (22)	=	say goodbye
dale (7)	=	valley	melodist (23)	=	musician
maidens (8)	=	girls	parching (30)	=	very dry

heifer (33)	=	young cow / calf
lowing (33)	=	mooing
morn (37)	=	morning
Attic (41)	=	Greek
brede (41)	=	interwoven pattern

What effect is achieved by this choice of words?

The poem appears to be very serious. The poet's description reflects his feelings when looking at the urn. He is elevated and that emotion is reflected in his elevated style.

Im Anschluss an diese Aufgabe sollten die Schülerinnen und Schüler die Strophen auf Stilmittel untersuchen und herausfinden, mit welchen anderen Mitteln Keats seine Begeisterung für das altgriechische Kunstwerk ausdrückt. Da es sich um ein recht langes Gedicht handelt, sollten sich die Schülerinnen und Schüler in fünf Gruppen ausführlich mit inhaltlichen und formalen Aspekten der fünf Strophen des Gedichtes befassen. Der Arbeitsauftrag lautet für alle Gruppen gleich.

We have looked at Keat's choice of words. Now say in one sentence what each stanza is about and find stylistic devices that the poet uses to underline his enthusiasm for the Greek urn.

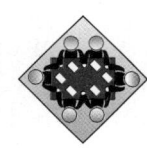

Die Lösungen sollten von den Gruppen selbst vorgetragen werden. Man kann ihnen Folien mit den einzelnen Strophen vorbereiten, mit deren Hilfe sie zunächst die stilistischen Aspekte und später dann das Reimschema und die metrische Analyse präsentieren können.
Die detaillierten Lösungsvorschläge finden sich im Anschluss an die folgende Aufgabe.

Having looked at the poem's content and language let us now analyse its rhyme scheme and metric pattern.

Notizen:

_____

_____

_____

_____

_____

_____

John Keats, *Ode on a Grecian Urn*

Thou still unravished bride of quietness!
Thou foster-child of silence and slow time,
Sylvan historian, who canst thus express
A flow'ry tale more sweetly than our rhyme:
5 What leaf-fringed legend haunts about thy shape
Of deities or mortals, or of both,
In Tempe or the dales of Arcady?
What men or gods are these? What maidens loth?
What mad pursuit? What struggle to escape?
10 What pipes and timbrels? What wild ecstasy?

Heard melodies are sweet, but those unheard
Are sweeter; therefore, ye soft pipes, play on;
Not to the sensual ear, but, more endeared,
Pipe to the spirit ditties of no tone:
15 Fair youth, beneath the trees, thou canst not leave
Thy song, nor ever can those trees be bare;
Bold Lover, never, never canst thou kiss,
Though winning near the goal – yet, do not grieve;
She cannot fade, though thou hast not thy bliss,
20 For ever wilt thou love, and she be fair!

Ah, happy, happy boughs! that cannot shed
Your leaves, nor ever bid the Spring adieu;
And, happy melodist, unwearied,
For ever piping songs for ever new;
25 More happy love! more happy, happy love!
For ever warm and still to be enjoyed,
For ever panting and for ever young;
All breathing human passion far above,
That leaves a heart high-sorrowful and cloyed,
30 A burning forehead, and a parching tongue.

Who are these coming to the sacrifice?
To what green altar, O mysterious priest,
Lead'st thou that heifer lowing at the skies,
And all her silken flanks with garlands drest?
35 What little town by river or sea-shore,
Or mountain-built with peaceful citadel,
Is emptied of its folk, this pious morn?
And, little town, thy streets for evermore
Will silent be; and not a soul to tell
40 Why thou art desolate, can e'er return.

---

unravished not carried off by force

Sylvan rustic, representing a woodland scene

Tempe valley in Greece
Arcady ideal valley
loth loath, unwilling

sensual ear ear of sense

ditties short, simple songs

bliss supreme happiness

boughs branches of tree

cloyed wearied by an excess of food/pleasure
parching very dry

heifer young cow
lowing mooing
drest dressed

© Schöningh Verlag, Best.-Nr. 041227-4

O Attic shape! Fair attitude! with brede
Of marble men and maidens overwrought,
With forest branches and the trodden weed;
Thou, silent form, dost tease us out of thought
45 As doth eternity: Cold pastoral!
When old age shall this generation waste,
Thou shalt remain, in midst of other woe
Than ours, a friend to man, to whom thou sayst,
"Beauty is truth, truth beauty, – that is all
50 Ye know on earth, and all ye need to know."

Attic Greek
brede interwoven pattern
overwrought elaborately decorated

woe grievous trouble

© Schöningh Verlag, Best.-Nr. 041227-4

First Stanza

This stanza is the introduction to the following reflection on the beauty of the urn.

Stylistic devices:

Thou ...

Thou ... (1/2)   =   anaphora stresses the address to the urn, the fact that the first line is an exclamation also contributes to the impression of enthusiasm

... express

a flow'ry. (3/4)   =   enjambement in order to stress the following list of questions

The following list of seven questions introduced by "what" emphasizes the narrator's puzzlement over the urn's secrets. This is also stressed by the expression "haunts" (l. 5).

The rhyme scheme is a, b, a, b, d, e, f, d, f, e

The metric pattern is iambic pentameter.

Second Stanza

This stanza is preoccupied with the sense of hearing. The poet likes the melodies that he can imagine when looking at the musicians on the urn better than real music of his day.

Stylistic devices:

In lines 11–14 Keats elaborates on a comparison between this unheard and real music. (heard – unheard; sensual ear – spirit)

The poet's enthusiasm for the urn is again stressed by repetition (nor ever l. 14, never, never l. 15, for ever l. 20).

Again the narrator addresses the depicted people by saying "fair youth" (l. 15) and "Bold Lover" (l. 17) and thus creates the impression of direct contact to the long-dead figures.

At the end of the stanza there is the contrast between the young girl who can never be kissed, which is a pity, and the almost fantastic fact that she will never become old. This contrast is also stressed by the alliteration "though thou hast not thy bliss" (l. 19).

The rhyme scheme is a, b, c, b, d, e, f, d, f, e. It is interesting to note that lines 1 and 3 form an eye-rhyme. Again this stresses the contrast between heard and imagined melodies.

The metric pattern is iambic pentameter.

Third Stanza

In this stanza the poet admires the perpetual spring that can be seen on the urn.

Stylistic devices:

The stanza starts with an exclamation and the repetition of the word "happy" (l. 21). This word is repeated again in lines 23, 25 (three times). This sets the tone of this stanza. The phrases "nor ever" and "forever" are also repeated several times (lines 22, 24, 26, 27), which again stress the narrator's longing for the Greeks' immortality which they attained by means of their art. He contrasts their happiness with the mortals' sorrows and occasional unhappiness and stresses this by using a chiasm in the last two lines:

"heart high-sorrowful and cloyed   noun – adjective
a burning forehead and a parching tongue"   adjective – noun

Again, there is an eye-rhyme in lines 21 / 23 (shed – unwearied).

The rhyme scheme is iambic pentameter, however, there is one exception in line 23 where the regular pattern is broken (= iambic tetrameter with feminine ending). In combination with the eye-rhyme you can assume that Keats wants to stress this line where he connects the two topics of the poem – happiness and melody.

Fourth Stanza

The fourth stanza deals with what cannot be seen on the urn, namely the homes of those who attend the sacrifice. The narrator speculates on where they live.

Stylistic devices:

This stanza starts with a question which also explains the topic of this part of the poem. The narrator speculates on where the depicted figures come from. He addresses the priest directly, which creates the impression that there is real communication.

The phrase "green altar" (l. 31) evokes an image of a population that lives in accordance with nature.

The contrast between the "town by river or sea-shore" and the "mountain-built" town shows that the narrator does not really know himself where these mysterious people on the urn come from and where their silent homes are.

The rhyme scheme is a, b, a, c, d, e, f, d, e, f.
The meter is iambic pentameter.

Fifth Stanza

This stanza connects the eternal beauty of the urn with the narrator's real life. He mourns the fact that he will perish whereas the beauty of the urn will "live" forever.

Stylistic devices:

The stanza starts with a direct address to the urn. This has the effect that the reader can imagine the urn and its beauty. This effect is heightened by the alliteration in line 42: "marble men and maidens".

The urn is compared with eternity, and both are very impressive.

Then the urn is addressed with an image: "cold pastoral" (l. 45). This sounds a bit like a paradox, because we think of warmth and green and peaceful pastures when we think of a pastoral. The adjective cold refers to the material of which the urn is made, namely marble.

The image of old age disposing of the narrator's generation stresses the eternity of the urn's beauty. It is even personified and called "friend to man" (l. 48).

The chiasm "beauty is truth, truth beauty" (l. 49) and the parallelism in line 50 "Ye know on earth and all ye need to know" underline the narrator's belief that nothing in the world is more important than beauty.

The rhyme scheme is a, b, a, b, c, d, e, d, c, e.
The meter is iambic pentameter.

Nach der Präsentation dieser Ergebnisse kann man eine Diskussion darüber anregen, mit welcher Absicht der Autor dieses Gedicht geschrieben hat. Man kann den Schülerinnen und Schülern sagen, dass Keats einer der bedeutendsten Vertreter der Romantik war und dass diese Gruppe von Dichtern besonders der Natur und ihrer Verherrlichung verpflichtet war. Die Begeisterung für die Kunst der alten Griechen und die Sehnsucht des Autors nach der antiken Idylle werden deutlich im Gedicht zum Ausdruck gebracht und sollten genannt werden. Zum Abschluss sollte ein Schüler / eine Schülerin das Gedicht zusammenhängend vortragen.

Nach der Erarbeitung dieses relativ langen Gedichts wird als Nächstes das Sonett behandelt. Um den Schülerinnen und Schülern beide Formen des Sonetts, das italienische und das elisabethanische, vorstellen zu können, wurden zwei entsprechende Sonette ausgewählt, zum einen William Shakespeares *Sonett 73* und danach John Miltons *Sonett VII*.

Beide Gedichte werden zugleich verteilt und sollen als Hausaufgabe auf ihr Reimschema untersucht werden.
Die Lösungen werden dann in der folgenden Unterrichtsstunde verglichen. Dabei wird sich der Unterschied im Reimschema herausstellen:

Read these two poems, find out what their rhyme schemes are and state how the content is affected.

The rhyme scheme of Shakespeare's sonnet is: a, b, a, b, c, d, c, d, e, f, e, f, g, g.
The rhyme scheme of Milton's sonnet reads: a, b, b, a, a, b, b, a, c, d, e, d, c, e.
The rhyme scheme is reflected in the content of both sonnets. In Shakespeare's sonnet there are three times four lines expressing different aspects of the topic age, the heroic couplet (last two lines) summing up his main concern.
In Milton's sonnet we find eight lines plus six lines, the first eight lines referring to his age, the last six lines referring to his outlook on his future.

What similarities do these two poems have?

A similarity is that both poems have 14 lines and both are written in iambic pentameters.

Nach der Erarbeitung dieser überwiegend formalen Aspekte folgt nun eine gründliche inhaltliche Interpretation dieser beiden Sonette. Es bietet sich eine arbeitsteilige Gruppenarbeit an. Jede Gruppe untersucht, inwieweit die durch das Reimschema vorgegebene Teilung der Sonette in vier bzw. zwei Abschnitte inhaltlich mitgetragen wird.

Notizen:

_____

_____

_____

_____

_____

_____

_____

_____

William Shakespeare, *Sonnet 73*

That time of year thou mayst in me behold   **behold** see
When yellow leaves, or none, or few, do hang
Upon those boughs which shake against the cold,
Bare ruined choirs where late the sweet birds sang.   **late** once, in earlier times
5 In me thou seest the twilight of such day
As after sunset fadeth in the west,   **fadeth** fades (two syllables)
Which by and by black night doth take away,
Death's second self, that seals up all in rest.
In me thou seest the glowing of such fire
10 That on the ashes of his youth doth lie,
As the death-bed whereon it must expire,
Consumed with that which it was nourished by.   **consumed** destroyed
This thou perceiv'st, which makes thy love more strong,   **perceiv'st** see
To love that well which thou must leave ere long.   **ere** before

John Milton, *Sonnet VII*

On His Being Arrived to the Age of Twenty-three

How soon hath Time, the subtle thief of youth,
Stol'n on his wing my three and twentieth year!
My hasting days fly on with full career,
But my late spring no bud or blossom shew'th.   **shew'th** shows
5 Perhaps my semblance might deceive the truth,
That I to manhood am arrived so near,
And inward ripeness doth much less appear,
That some more timely-happy spirits indu'th.   **indu'th** endoweth = to equip
Yet be it less or more, or soon or slow,
10 It shall be still in strictest measure ev'n   **ev'n** equal, adequate
To that same lot, however mean or high,
Toward which Time leads me, and the will of Heav'n;
All is, if I have grace to use it so,
As ever in my great Task-master's eye.

© Schöningh Verlag, Best.-Nr. 041227-4

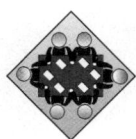

You have identified the rhyme scheme of this poem. Now look at its content and find out if rhyme scheme and content correspond.

Paraphrase what each part of your sonnet is about and try to identify and explain stylistic devices the author uses.

William Shakespeare, *Sonnet 73*

In this sonnet the author deals with the end of his life which is approaching. In the first four stanzas the narrator describes an autumn day with all its signs of decay: The trees are losing their leaves and the birds are no longer singing. He addresses a person and compares the autumn day to himself. ("thou mayst in me behold", l. 1)

In order to underline the gloomy atmosphere the author uses an enumeration in line 2: "yellow leaves, or none, or few" which reflects the narrator's sadness about the end of the year because it is quite illogical. The enjambement in lines 3/4 stresses the enumeration of how desolate the choir is in contrast to the sweetness of the birds.

In the next four stanzas the narrator compares himself to the end of a day. The beauty of a day and sunlight is contrasted with "black night" (l. 7). Again he addresses someone.

This contrast is underlined by the alliteration "by and by black" (l. 7). The night is called "death's second self" (l. 8), an expression that is usually connected to sleep, however, since the narrator is really talking about the end of his life this allusion fits the purpose to evoke the image of approaching death.

In the next quadruplet the narrator speaks about his own death-bed. He talks about the "ashes" of his fire when he was young and he says that this fire is destroyed by what it used to feed on. Whether he wants to reflect on the damaging effects of his doings as a younger man or on the fact that everybody is eventually consumed by the effort it takes to live remains open to discussion. The contrasting words "consumed" – "nourished" (l. 12) underline the contrast between summer – autumn, day – night, and life – death.

The fact that this is addressed to a person is underlined by the repeated expression "in me thou seest" (ll. 5 and 9).

In the last two verses, the heroic couplet, the narrator again speaks to the unknown person, he sums up the last 12 lines with "This thou perceiv'st" (l. 13) and then goes on to draw his conclusion from what he has stated before. He thinks that this person's love must become stronger because he or she now knows that he, the narrator, will not live much longer.

John Milton, *Sonnet VII*

In this poem Milton reflects on his life and how fast his first 23 years have passed. In the first eight lines he thinks about the swift passage of his lifetime so far. He personifies time and calls it a "thief of youth" (l. 1), then he carries on the metaphor and says that time has stolen his life on "wings" (l. 2). The metaphor is then twisted and applied to his "hasting days" (l. 3) which "fly" (l. 3) away. In this way these three lines introduce the poet's theme, namely his lament about how fast our lives pass and the fact that sometimes the passing of time does not correspond with inner development.

He calls his present age "late spring" (l. 4) that has neither "bud or blossom" (l. 4). This metaphor evokes the image of a still young man who, however, no longer indulges in youth's folly. The alliteration in "bud or blossom" underlines that although fun is over signs of inner ripeness do not yet show. He thinks he looks much younger than he is and that his inner maturity does not yet show in his outward appearance. The "timely-happy spirits" (l. 8) that have given him this inner ripeness are stressed by an irregularity in the meter; the line reads:

U — U — U— U—U U —

That some more timely-happy spirits indu'th

The anapest hastens the verse and conveys the image of lively spirits.
In the last six lines the author reflects on the consequences of the above stated fact. He uses antithetical expressions to underline his trust in God who will receive him at the end of his life: less or more, or soon or slow (l. 9). Again time is personified as his leader that will together with heaven's will bring him to his fate. He trusts that if he uses his belief his fate will be in his "Task-master's eye" (l. 14). The phrase task-master personifies God as the active leader of our lives and thus shows the poet's deep belief in God.

Um die Unterschiede der Reimschemata noch einmal deutlich zu machen bietet es sich an, diese in einem Tafelbild festzuhalten.

As we have seen, different rhyme schemes are used in these two sonnets. There are two kinds of sonnets, the Italian or Petrarchan Sonnet (Milton) and the Elizabethan or Shakespearean Sonnet. Name their rhyme schemes:

Italian / Petrarchan		Elizabethan / Shakespearean	
a		a	
b		b	
b		a	
a		b	four lines (quatrain)
a		c	
b		d	
b		c	
a	eight lines (octave)	d	four lines
c		e	
d		f	
c		e	
d		f	four lines
c		g	
d	six lines (sestet)	g	two lines (heroic couplet)

Nach der Beschäftigung mit Gedichten aus vergangenen Jahrhunderten sollen nun zeitgenössische Dichter mit moderner Ausdrucksweise zu Wort kommen.
In einem kurzen Lehrervortrag kann man die Schülerinnen und Schüler darüber informieren, dass sich in diesem Jahrhundert die zuvor kennen gelernten Formen der Poesie aufgelöst haben und es heute andere Formen der Dichtung gibt, in denen immer noch die Zusammenstellung der Wörter einen Rhythmus ergibt, dieser aber nicht mehr unbedingt in Reimschemata und festen metrischen Formen gebunden ist. Alternativ kann man ihnen aber auch die Kopiervorlage *Free Verse* aushändigen und sie selbst untersuchen lassen, inwieweit diese Gedichte sich von den bisher gelesenen unterscheiden.

Let us now have a look at a more modern kind of poetry – free verse. In the 20th century poets rejected the traditional forms more and more. They started to experiment with new forms. Eventually a poem could be written without a set rhyme scheme or metrical pattern. However, these poems also have a rhythm based on our natural speech rhythm which is expressed in the use of lines and spaces to indicate pauses. These poems rely on their arrangement of words and surprising metaphors. Good examples of this kind of poetry are *This is Just to Say* and *The Red Wheelbarrow* by William Carlos Williams.

Nach dieser Vorinformation können die Schülerinnen und Schüler sich in häuslicher Arbeit mit der Fragestellung auseinander setzen, weshalb diese Texte als Gedichte bezeichnet werden können.

Although a rhyme scheme or metrical pattern cannot be identified, these two texts are certainly poems. Why? What do these poems describe? What situations can you imagine?

This is Just to Say could be a note left on a kitchen table, or a message on an answering machine. It conveys that the relationship between the speaker and the person the note is addressed to is a good one because the speaker obviously expects the forgiveness he is asking for to be granted. Maybe the speaker had to leave early for work or a trip and was not able to resist the temptation of the plums in the fridge or another cool place in the kitchen. He takes into consideration his partner's being angry about the "stolen" plums and tries to explain his appetite.

The Red Wheelbarrow has no obvious meaning. It does not tell a story, but describes a thing that has attracted the speaker's attention. The wheelbarrow's beauty standing on a farm wet from the rain is the topic of the poem. Thus, the important thing for the author is not to reflect on anything, but simply to express beauty in an everyday occurrence, and so he wants to sharpen his readers' senses to these beautiful things that surround us without our noticing them. The question "what does it mean" is not at all appropriate here.

Notizen:

_____

_____

_____

_____

_____

_____

_____

_____

_____

Free Verse

William Carlos Williams, *This is Just to Say*

I have eaten
the plums
that were in
the icebox

5 and which
you were probably
saving
for breakfast

Forgive me
10 they were delicious
so sweet
and so cold

William Carlos Williams, *The Red Wheelbarrow*

so much depends
upon

a red wheel
barrow

5 glazed with rain
water

beside the white
chickens

D. H. Lawrence, *To Women, As Far As I'm Concerned*

The feelings I don't have I don't have.
The feelings I don't have, I won't say I have.
The feelings you say you have, you don't have.
The feelings you would like us both to have, we neither of us have.
5 The feelings people ought to have, they never have.
If people say they've got feelings, you may be pretty sure they haven't got them.
So if you want either of us to feel anything at all
you'd better abandon all ideas of feelings altogether.

© Schöningh Verlag, Best.-Nr. 041227-4

Das dritte Gedicht auf der Kopiervorlage, D. H. Lawrences *To Women, As Far As I'm Concerned,* ist ebenfalls ein Beispiel für die *Free Verse*-Technik. Lawrence beschreibt sein Verhältnis zu Frauen. Die Schülerinnen und Schüler sollten das Gedicht auf seinen Rhythmus untersuchen und versuchen in eigenen Worten zu beschreiben, welche Einstellung des Sprechers zu Frauen in dem Gedicht zutage tritt.

Explain what attitude D. H. Lawrence seems to have towards women. How does he use free verse to convey his message?

In his poem D. H. Lawrence talks about the feelings he has or does not have for women. He shows how false many of our utterings about feelings towards our partners are. He not only makes clear that he does not want to pretend to have feelings he does not feel. He also deeply mistrusts the words of women who pretend to have feelings for him. He seems to think that talking about feelings destroys the ability to have feelings at all. He seems to think that our general ideas about feelings (l. 9) have nothing to do with what he regards as feeling. The constant repetition of "The feelings" at the beginning of the first 5 lines sets the tone of the poem without any rhyme scheme or definite metrical pattern. Rhythm is created by repetition of sentence structure, too. Thus, the first two lines deal with "I", the next two with "you", then he starts to talk about people in line 5. So far the lines are rather short. But then he ends the poem with two very long sentences which leave the reader breathless. The antithetical ideas of people stating that they have feelings, the poet's conviction that they do not have them, and the paradoxical statement that you have to abandon any idea of feeling before you can feel anything underline his message to beware of paying lip service.

Nach der Besprechung dieser Aufgabe sollen die Schülerinnen und Schüler kurz Bekanntschaft mit einer der letzten großen Balladen des 20. Jahrhunderts machen. Oscar Wildes *Ballad of Reading Goal,* verfasst während seiner Gefängnishaft, ist erheblich zu lang, um ganz besprochen zu werden, allerdings kann man sich sehr wohl mit einem Ausschnitt beschäftigen. Gewählt wurde der Anfang der Ballade. Bevor der Text ausgeteilt und gelesen wird, können einige *pre-reading*-Aufgaben das sicherlich bereits vorhandene Wissen der Schülerinnen und Schüler zum Thema Ballade aktivieren.

What ballads did you read in your German lessons? What are they about?

Je nach Deutschunterricht können hier z. B. Schillers Balladen oder auch der Erlkönig genannt werden. Es sollte herausgearbeitet werden, dass diese Balladen volkstümliche Inhalte transportieren oder von heldenhaften Handlungen berichten. Nach diesem Exkurs wird nun der Text verteilt.

Notizen:

_____

_____

_____

_____

Oscar Wilde, *The Ballad of Reading Goal*

He did not wear his scarlet coat,
For blood and wine are red
And blood and wine were on his hands
When they found him with the dead,
5 The poor dead woman whom he loved,
And murdered in her bed.

He walked amongst the Trial Men
in a suit of shabby grey;
A cricket cap was on his head,
10 And his step seemed light and gay;
But I never saw a man who looked
So wistfully at the day.

wistful characterised by melancholy, longing, yearning

I never saw a man who looked
with such a wistful eye
15 Upon that little tent of blue
Which prisoners call the sky,
And at every drifting cloud that went
With sails of silver by.

I walked, with other souls in pain,
20 Within another ring,
And was wondering if the man had done
A great or little thing,
When a voice behind me whispered low,
"That fellow' got to swing."

25 Dear Christ! the very prison walls
Suddenly seemed to reel,
And the sky above my head became
Like a casque of scorching steel;
And, though I was a soul in pain,
30 My pain I could not feel.

to reel to sway or rock under a blow, shock

casque a helmet
to scorch to burn surface with flame or heat

I only knew what hunted thought
Quickened his step, and why
He looked upon the garish day
With such a wistful eye;
35 The man had killed the thing he loved,
And so he had to die.

garish crudely or tastelessly colourful, excessively ornate

© Schöningh Verlag, Best.-Nr. 041227-4

Die erste Frage sollte sich wiederum auf den Inhalt beziehen, anschließend können die rhythmischen Besonderheiten der Ballade erörtert werden.

What is this ballad about? Analyse the rhyme scheme and metrical pattern.

In this first part of a long ballad Wilde describes a man who he meets in prison and who has been convicted of murder and is about to be hanged. The author describes this man's unhappy appearance and expresses his shock when he learns that this fellow-prisoner is going to die.

The rhyme scheme is quite unusual. In each stanza only three lines rhyme: a, b, c, b, d, b. The iambic meter is also often broken. There is usually a iambic tetrameter followed by a iambic trimeter, however, there are many variations with anapests, e. g. first stanza fourth line starts with an anapest:

U   U   —   U   —   U   —
When they found him with the dead

Can you explain in which way this text is typical of a ballad? Bear in mind that ballads were popular in a time when mass media were not available to people.

There is a frequent repetition of words which makes it easier to follow the content of the text. In the first stanza *blood and wine* are repeated (ll. 2 / 3) and *dead* (ll. 4 / 5) and the fact that the woman is not only dead but has been murdered is mentioned in line 6.
Again there is a repetition in stanzas two and three of *wistful(ly)*. In the last stanza the expressions *wistful* and *kill* and *die* are taken up again.

Can you think of differences to the traditional ballad?

In a traditional ballad a story is told without the narrator reflecting on or expressing any emotions. In this poem the narrator shows his deep emotions.

Wenn die Schülerinnen und Schüler dies erkannt haben, kann in Partnerarbeit von ihnen herausgefunden werden, welche Gefühle der Erzähler ausdrückt und welche stilistischen Mittel dafür eingesetzt werden.

What feelings does the narrator express and which stylistic devices does the author use to convey them?

The author expresses emotions not only when he learns about the convicted man's fate, but also when he informs the reader about his own experiences in prison. He calls the sky "that little tent of blue" (l. 15) and clouds have "sails of silver" (l. 18). These expressions show that the prisoner is perhaps dreaming of freedom or heaven or is simply admiring the beauty of nature and thus tries to escape from the monotony and boredom of prison days. He says that he and the others are "souls in pain" (l. 19). Here it becomes clear how terrible the situation is for the narrator. In the fifth stanza the narrator shows deep emotion at the news that one of his friends will be executed. It starts with an exclamation "Dear Christ!" (l. 25), his shock is reflected by the fact that the prison walls seem to shake and the little tent of blue is now a "casque of scorching steel" (l. 28), a metaphor that clearly shows pain. He is numb with pain: "My pain I could not feel" (l. 30).

Im Anschluss an die Besprechung dieser Gedichte kann man den Schülerinnen und Schülern die Kopiervorlage zu den *stylistic devices* und die Handreichung *How to interpret a poem* aushändigen.

Nach Erarbeitung dieses *Component* sollte nun ausgewählt werden, welche Themenkomplexe man weiter besprechen möchte.

Notizen:

_____

_____

_____

_____

_____

_____

_____

_____

_____

_____

_____

_____

_____

_____

_____

_____

Stylistic Devices and Forms of Poetry

alliteration:	repetition of speech sounds, usually consonants, in a sequence of words that are close together
allusion:	reference to a well-known person, place, or event, or to another literary work or passage
anaphora:	repetition of a word or expression at the beginning of phrases, sentences or verses
ballad:	originally a song, transmitted orally, which tells a story, later a narrative poem
cliché:	stereotype, expression that has been used so often that it has become commonplace
euphemism:	the use of a vague term for something disagreeable or offensive
free verse:	printed like poetry, but without rhyme or regular syllabic stress pattern
metaphor:	a figure of speech in which a word phrase literally denoting one kind of object in place of another to suggest a likeness
ode:	a long lyric poem that is serious in subject and elevated in style
parallelism:	recurrent syntactical similarities introduced for rhetorical effect
personification:	attribution of personal qualities to an inanimate object
simile:	figure of speech comparing two unlike things, often introduced by *like* or *as*
sonnet:	a fixed verse form: fourteen lines usually (3 x 4 + 1 x 2 or 1 x 8 + 1 x 6)
symbol:	a word or phrase that signifies an object

© Schöningh Verlag, Best.-Nr. 041227-4

How to interpret a poem

Ask yourself the following questions:
- What sort of poem is it? (narrative; descriptive, *Ode to Grecian Urn;* reflective, *Life Sculpture*)
- Who is speaking, who is being addressed?
- What is the poem about? What meaning does the title have?
- What is the author's intention?
- What is the predominant mood?

Look at the vocabulary of the poem: theme, words (adjectives, verbs, etc.), register

Look at the syntactical structure:
long / short sentences
questions, exclamations
repetitions, parallelism, antithesis
enjambements, caesuras

Analyse the poem's
- rhythm
- rhyme / sound effects
- stylistic devices

Now you can start writing your interpretation:

Introduction
You should always start with an introductory sentence giving the poet's name, the title of the poem and if possible the genre, when it was published and what it is about.

Main Part
Explain by close analysis how the poet expresses his ideas and what effect they have on the reader.
You should organise your material and divide your text into paragraphs, each dealing with one aspect of the poem.

Conclusion
A short appreciation of the poem. You should state briefly how convincing the poet has been in connecting form and content.

© Schöningh Verlag, Best.-Nr. 041227-4

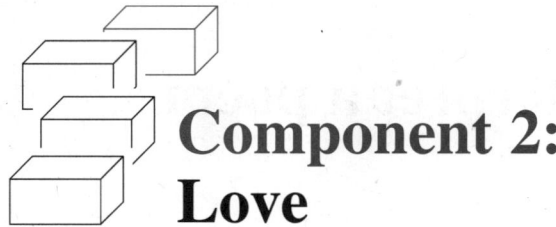

Component 2: Love

In diesem ersten thematischen *Component* geht es um Gedichte aus dem Themengebiet „Liebe". Zunächst soll ein Gedicht besprochen werden, in dem ein lyrischer Sprecher seine Angebetete versucht zu überreden, sich ihm hinzugeben. Diese Überredung ist in ironisch-leichtem Ton abgefasst und ist somit auch heute noch, über 300 Jahre nach Entstehen des Gedichtes (1681), ausgesprochen unterhaltsam. Es empfiehlt sich wiederum, das Gedicht auf eine Overhead-Folie zu kopieren und mit Folienstiften die Ergebnisse der Analyse eintragen zu lassen. Eine detaillierte Lösung der Aufgaben zu diesem längeren Gedicht findet sich auf dem *Solution sheet*. Bevor man ausführlich Reimschema, Metrik und die Stilmittel analysiert, sollte die Frage nach dem Inhalt des Textes gestellt werden.

▌ What is this poem about?

▌ In this poem a man who is in love with a young woman tries to convince her to make love to him.

In einer arbeitsgleichen Gruppenarbeit sollten die Schülerinnen und Schüler sich genauer mit dem Inhalt des Gedichtes auseinander setzen. Dabei kann eine Einteilung dieses langen Gedichtes in Abschnitte helfen. Ein Tafelbild visualisiert die Ergebnisse. Danach sollte das Augenmerk des Kurses zunächst auf die metrischen Unregelmäßigkeiten und dann auf die literarischen Stilmittel, die Marvell benutzt, gelenkt werden. Typischerweise für die Dichtung kann man hierbei Metaphern, Vergleiche und Kontraste finden und die metrischen Unregelmäßigkeiten in Verbindung mit dem Inhalt setzen.

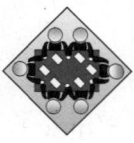

▌ Divide this poem into several parts and describe what these parts are about in your own words.

ll. 1–20	the narrator expresses his wish to have endless time to woo his beloved
ll. 21–32	he has fear of time catching up and ruining beauty and love
ll. 33–46	he strongly wishes to make love to the young woman, wants to devour time and not be beaten by it

▌ When reading this poem out loud you realize that its rhyme and meter are not as regular as it looks at first sight. Can you identify the irregularities?

▌ There are three couplets (two rhyming lines) that look like rhymes, but happen not to rhyme when read out loud.

Andrew Marvell, *To His Coy Mistress*

Had we but world enough and time,
This coyness, lady, were no crime.
We would sit down and think which way
To walk, and pass our long love's day.

5 Thou by the Indian Ganges' side
Shouldst rubies find: I by the tide
Of Humber would complain. I would
Love you ten years before the Flood;
And you should, if you please, refuse

10 Till the conversion of the Jews.
My vegetable love should grow
Vaster than empires, and more slow.
An hundred years should go to praise
Thine eyes, and on thy forehead gaze;

15 Two hundred to adore each breast,
But thirty thousand to the rest;
An age at least to every part,
And the last age should show your heart.
For, lady, you deserve this state;

20 Nor would I love at lower rate.
But at my back I always hear
Time's winged chariot hurrying near;
And yonder all before us lie
Deserts of vast eternity.

25 Thy beauty shall no more be found
Nor, in thy marble vault, shall sound
My echoing song; then worms shall try
That long-preserved virginity;
And your quaint honour turn to dust,

30 And into ashes all my lust.
The grave's a fine and private place,
But none, I think, do there embrace.
Now, therefore, while the youthful hue
Sits on thy skin like morning dew,

35 And while thy willing soul transpires
At every pore with instant fires,
Now let us sport us while we may,
And now, like am'rous birds of prey,
Rather at once our time devour

40 Than languish in his slow-chapped pow'r.
Let us roll all our strength and all
Our sweetness up into one ball,
And tear our pleasures with rough strife
Thorough the iron gates of life.
Thus, though we cannot make our sun
Stand still, yet we will make him run.

coyness modesty

Humber muddy river that runs through Hull

thine / thy your

state dignity

chariot two wheeled vehicle

vault burial chamber

quaint unusual in an interesting way

hue colour

transpires breathes forth
instant fires enthusiasm

birds of prey flesh-eating bird like eagle
devour to eat up hungrily
languish to lose vitality
slow-chapped slow-jawed

strife strenuous effort

Andrew Marvell, *To His Coy Mistress* (Solution sheet)

Had we but world enough and time,
This coyness, lady, were no crime.
We would sit down and *think which way*
To walk, and pass our long love's day.
5 Thou by the Indian *Ganges' side*
Shouldst rubies find: I by the tide
Of Humber would complain. *I <u>would</u>*   = eye-rhyme
Love you ten years before the <u>Flood;</u>
And you should, if you please, *refuse*
10 *Till the conversion of the Jews.*
My vegetable love should grow
Vaster than empires, and more slow.
An hundred years should go *to praise*
Thine eyes, and on thy forehead gaze;
15 Two hundred to adore each breast,
But thirty thousand to the rest;
An age at least to every part,
And the last age should show your heart.
For, lady, you deserve this state;
20 Nor would I love at lower rate.
But at my back I *always hear*
Time's winged chariot hurrying near;
And yonder all *before us <u>lie</u>*   = eye-rhyme
Deserts of vast <u>eternity.</u>
25 Thy beauty shall no more be found
Nor, in thy marble vault, *shall sound*
My echoing song; then worms shall <u>try</u>   = eye-rhyme
That long-preserved <u>virginity;</u>
And your quaint honour turn to dust,
30 And into ashes all my lust.
The grave's a fine and private place,
But none, I think, do there embrace.
Now, therefore, while the *youthful hue*
Sits on thy skin like morning dew,
35 And while thy willing *soul transpires*
At every pore with instant fires,
Now let us sport us while we may,
And now, like am'rous birds of prey,
Rather at once our time *devour*
40 *Than languish* in his slow-chapped pow'r.
Let us roll all our strength *and all*
Our sweetness up into one ball,
And tear our pleasures with *rough strife*
Thorough the iron gates of life.
45 Thus, though we *cannot make our sun*
Stand still, yet we will make him run.

Bei den kursiv gedruckten Zeilen handelt sich um enjambements.

1. ll. 7 / 8   would – Flood
2. ll. 23 / 24   lie   – eternity
3. ll. 27 / 28   try   – virginity

These rhymes are called **eye-rhymes.**

Sometimes a sentence does not stop at the end of a line, but runs on, as in lines 5–8:

Thou by the Indian Ganges' side
Shouldst rubies find: I by the tide
Of Humber would complain. I would
Love you ten years before the Flood;

These run-on lines are called **enjambements.**

Why is this poem full of enjambements?

This poem has a very regular rhyme scheme and meter, so these variations are needed to make it more interesting. The enjambements especially help to prevent the reader from falling into a monotone reading.

What stylistic devices does the author use to make this poem interesting?

Throughout the poem we find metaphors of time. In the first part of the poem there are many exaggerations referring to the time the narrator would like to have to woo his beloved (ll. 7–9). From line 13 on he names enormous amounts of times he would like to dedicate to his love (ll. 13–18). Here the image of time is interwoven with a geographical comparison between the immense Ganges in India and the humble river Humber in Hull. This contrast underlines the narrator's main contrast between the time he would like to have and the actual short time that he and the maiden have to enjoy life and love.
In the second part he warns the girl of time that is rushing on (l. 22: Time's winged chariot) that will eventually destroy her beauty and their love and interest in each other. In this part the author also evokes images of the grave and death. He is very outspoken in this (l. 26: marble vault; l. 27: worms; l. 29: honour to dust; l. 30: lust to ashes) and tries to scare her.
In the last part of the poem he urges her to ignore time's progress and to hurry with him to fulfil their love, so that time, the slow-chapped power (l. 40) is defeated. This expression is underlined by the use of a simile. The poem ends with a paradox, namely that time, which cannot be stopped, is itself chased.

Nach der Untersuchung des Gedichtes werden die Schülerinnen und Schüler nun aufgefordert, einen Zusammenhang zwischen den metrischen Unregelmäßigkeiten und dem Inhalt des Gedichtes herzustellen. Diese Aufgabe eignet sich als Hausaufgabe.

Can you explain why certain irregularities in the metric pattern appear?

The first eye-rhyme (ll. 7/8) is coupled with a long enjambement (ll. 5–10), this is probably the case because here the image of time is introduced for the first time.

53

A very irregular metric pattern can be found in line 22:

Time's winged chariot hurrying near

instead of the iambic meter we read

——U I U —— I U ——I U ——

This metric deviation used in the central line of the poem where the narrator tries to scare his beloved into submitting to him demonstrates how form and content can correspond in good poetry.

Auch das folgende Gedicht von W. H. Auden behandelt das Thema Liebe, jedoch lesen wir hier eine Lebensgeschichte, die geprägt ist von enttäuschter Liebe und die ein tragisches Ende findet. Das Gedicht ist eine Ballade, daher lässt es sich leicht vortragen. Jedoch sollte man wegen der Länge des Gedichtes nicht nur eine(n) Schüler(in), sondern mehrere den Text vortragen lassen. Bei der Länge des Gedichts muss man der Klasse Zeit lassen, den Inhalt wiederzugeben.

Als Hausaufgabe kann man das Gedicht zu Hause vorbereiten und kurz zusammenfassen lassen, wovon es handelt.

What is the poem *Victor* about?

This poem is about the life of a man called Victor who leads a rather boring and uninteresting life until he meets a young woman. He falls in love and marries her not realizing that she has had affairs with most of his colleagues. When he finds out about her past he kills her in a fit of jealousy. This poem is a ballad.

Nach der kurzen Rekapitulation des Inhalts zu Beginn der folgenden Stunde kann man dazu übergehen, den Text genauer zu analysieren. Dabei empfiehlt es sich, die Schülerinnen und Schüler zunächst aufzufordern, den Text in Abschnitte einzuteilen und diese Abschnitte mit Überschriften und kurzen Inhaltsangaben zu versehen. Dies kann in Partnerarbeit erfolgen.

Divide the text into parts, find headings for these parts and summarize shortly the contents of these parts.

Notizen:

_____

_____

_____

_____

_____

_____

W. H. Auden, *Victor*

Victor was a little baby,
Into this world he came;
His father took him on his knee and said:
"Don't dishonour the family name."

5 Victor looked up at his father
Looked up with big round eyes:
His father said: "Victor, my only son,
Don't you ever ever tell lies."

Victor and his father went riding
10 Out in a little dog-cart;   **dog-cart** small open carriage
His father took a Bible from his pocket and read,   with two wheels
"Blessed are the pure in heart."

It was a frosty December,
It wasn't the season for fruits;
15 His father fell dead of heart disease
While lacing up his boots.

It was a frosty December
When into his grave his sank;
His uncle found Victor a post as cashier
20 In the Midland Counties Bank.

It was a frosty December
Victor was only eighteen,
But his figures were neat and his margins straight
And his cuffs were always clean.   **cuffs** band at the end of a
     sleeve

25 He took a room at the Peveril,
A respectable boarding house;
And Time watched Victor day after day
As a cat will watch a mouse.

The clerks slapped Victor on the shoulder;
30 "Have you ever had a woman?" they said,
"Come down town with us on Saturday night."
Victor smiled and shook his head.

The manager sat in his office,
Smoked a Corona cigar:
35 Said: "Victor is a decent fellow but
He's too mousy to go far."   **mousy** plain and quiet

Victor went up to his bedroom,
Set the alarum bell;
Climbed into bed, took his Bible and read
40 Of what happened to Jezebel.

alarum alarm

It was the First of April,
Anna to the Peveril came;
Her eyes, her lips, her breasts, her hips
And her smile set men aflame.

45 She looked as pure as a schoolgirl
On her First Communion day,
But her kisses were like the best champagne
When she gave herself away.

It was the Second of April,
50 She was wearing a coat of fur;
Victor met her upon the stairs
And he fell in love with her.

The first time he made his proposal,
She laughed, said: "I'll never wed":
55 The second time there was a pause;
Then she smiled and shook her head.

wed to marry

Anna looked into her mirror,
Pouted and gave a frown:
Said: "Victor's as dull as a wet afternoon
60 But I've got to settle down."

pouted to thrust out lips
dull slow of understanding

The third time he made his proposal,
As they walked by the Reservoir:
She gave him a kiss like a blow on the head.
Said: "You are my heart's desire."

65 They were married early in August,
She said: "Kiss me, you funny boy":
Victor took her in his arms and said;
"O my Helen of Troy."

It was the middle of September,
70 Victor came to the office one day;
He was wearing a flower in his buttonhole,
He was late but he was gay.

The clerks were talking of Anna,
The door was just ajar:
75 One said: "Poor old Victor, but where ignorance
Is a bliss, et cetera."

Victor stood still as a statue,
The door was just ajar:
One said: "God, what fun I had with her
80 In that Baby Austin car."

Victor walked out into the High Street,
He walked to the edge of town;
He came to the allotments and the rubbish heap;
And his tears came tumbling down.

85 Victor looked up at the sunset
As he stood there all alone;
Cried; "Are you in Heaven, Father?"
But the sky said "Address not known."

Victor looked up at the mountains,
90 The mountains all covered with snow;
Cried; "Are you pleased with me, Father?"
And the answer came back, "No."

Victor came to the forest,
Cried; "Father, will she ever be true?"
95 And the oaks and the beeches shook their heads
And they answered; "Not to you."

Victor came to the meadow
Where the wind went sweeping by:
Cried; "O Father, I love her so,"
100 But the wind said; "She must die."

Victor came to the river
Running so deep and so still,
Cried; "O Father, what shall I do?"
And the river answered; "Kill."

105 Anna was sitting at table
Drawing cards from a pack;
Anna was sitting at table
Waiting for her husband to come back.

It wasn't the Jack of Diamonds
110 Nor the joker she drew at first;

It wasn't the King or the Queen of Hearts
But the Ace of Spades reversed.

Victor stood in the doorway,
He didn't utter a word:
115 She said: "What's the matter darling?"
He behaved as if he hadn't heard.

There was a voice in his left ear,
There was a voice in his right,
There was a voice at the base of his skull
120 Saying: "She must die tonight."

Victor picked up a carving-knife,
His features were set and drawn,
Said: "Anna, it would have been better for you
If you had not been born."

125 Anna jumped up from the table,
Anna started to scream,
But Victor came slowly after her
Like a horror in a dream.

She dodged behind the sofa,   **dodge** to move suddenly aside
130 She tore down a curtain rod,
But Victor came slowly after her:
Said: "Prepare to meet thy God."   **thy** your

She managed to wrench the door open,
She ran and she didn't stop.
135 But Victor followed her up the stairs
And he caught her at the top.

He stood there above the body,
He stood there holding the knife;
And the blood ran down the stairs and sang;
140 "I'm the Resurrection and the Life."   **Resurrection** rising from the dead

They tapped Victor on the shoulder,
They took him away in a van;
He sat as quiet as a lump of moss
Saying; "I am the Son of Man."

145 Victor sat in a corner
Making a woman of clay:
Saying; "I am Alpha and Omega, I shall come
To judge the earth one day."

Part One:
Stanzas 1–6: Victor's youth
Auden tells the reader about Victor's birth and the main ideas his father has about how to live, namely to honour the family name (l. 4) and never to tell a lie (l. 8). Obviously Victor's father was a religious man (ll. 11/12). One winter his father dies of a heart disease (l. 15) and Victor starts to work as a clerk in bank (ll. 19/20).

Part Two:
Stanzas 7–10: Life as a clerk
The following 4 stanzas tell us about Victor's life at the office. He does not join his colleagues in their immoral life visiting bars on Saturday nights. Instead Victor spends his nights at home reading his Bible.

Part Three:
Stanzas 11–17: Meeting Anna
Victor meets Anna who moves into the same boarding house where he lives. He is fascinated by her and falls in love with her right away. He has to propose three times to her before she finally decides to marry him. Whereas he is very much in love, her reason for marrying him is that she feels a need to settle down.

Part Four:
Stanzas 18–20: Disillusion
Victor learns by chance that his wife had affairs with some of his colleagues and that she is not the pure young woman he has imagined her to be.

Part Five:
Stanzas 21–26: Victor's despair
Victor turns to nature to find an answer to his question what he should do now. He thinks that his father is disgusted by him and that the wind and the river order him to kill his wife.

Part Six:
Stanzas 27–34: The murder
Victor goes home to his wife and stabs her to death although she tries to run away from him. He does not show any mercy towards her.

Part Seven:
Stanzas 35–37: After the killing
After the murder of his wife Victor is apprehended and taken to prison. His last thoughts deal with religion. He feels he has had every right to kill his wife because of her immoral lifestyle.

Nach dieser genaueren Untersuchung des Inhalts des Gedichtes kann man dazu übergehen zu analysieren, wie Auden die verschiedenen Abschnitte in Victors Leben darstellt. Dies soll anhand von Interpretationen der einzelnen Abschnitte erfolgen. Bei dieser Interpretation soll jeweils darauf geachtet werden, inwieweit Elemente der Ballade eingesetzt werden. Diese Aufgabenstellung eignet sich wiederum für eine Gruppenarbeit. Die Ergebnisse dieser Arbeit können dann im Plenum vorgestellt werden.

Let us have a look at each of the poem's parts. How is Victor's life described? What stylistic devices are used to make clear to the reader what kind of life Victor leads? Identify elements that are typical of a ballad.

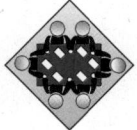

Part One:

We do not learn anything about Victor's mother. She does not seem to have had much influence on him. His father, on the other hand, seems to have been very important to him. His first command to his son is not to dishonour the family name. Next, Victor is admonished not to tell lies. This command is stressed by the repetitions in the second stanza "looked up" (ll. 5/6) and "ever" (l. 8). His father educates him in a religious way, which can be seen in stanza three when the father reads from the Bible. It is important that his quotation is "Blessed are the pure in heart" (l. 12). The shock that his father's death presents for Victor is stressed by the repetition of "It was a frosty December" as the first line of stanzas 4, 5 and 6. This is a typical element of a ballad which originally was not written down but told, so repetitions helped the listeners to follow the story.

Part Two:

There is no information about Victor's life at school, but we learn that he finds a job in an office where he works steadily but without any ambition or prospect of a career. His life is described by how others perceive him. First there is an interesting personification in stanza 7: "Time" (l. 27) watches Victor, and the comparison of a cat watching a mouse (l. 28) foreshadows the facts that Victor will be a victim.

In stanza 8 his colleagues are described as shoulder-slapping chaps who try to lure Victor to nightlife and women. However, Victor refuses to submit to their immoral ways.

Again he is compared with a mouse when his boss calls him "mousy" (l. 36). Instead of going out with his colleagues he goes home every night and reads his Bible. He reads the story of Jezebel who was, according to the Old Testament, the wife of King Ahab and became the archetype of the wicked woman because she interfered with the exclusive worship of the Hebrew god Yaweh. Again, by mentioning this biblical person Auden foreshadows events to come. Direct speech is another typical element of ballads which were recited publicly to entertain so they had to tell their stories in a lively way.

Part Three:

In stanza 11 there is an enumeration, which is a typical element of a ballad, combined with an internal thyme ("her lips ... her hips" l. 43). This stylistic device underlines the impression that Anna made on Victor. In stanza 12 we learn something about her. Although she looks like a schoolgirl her kisses are like the best champagne. The contrast of these comparisons stresses the fact that Anna looks innocent and thus would make an appropriate partner for Victor, but that she really has a different character. Again we come across an element that is often found in ballads, namely the anaphora of "It was the First of April" (l. 41) and "It was the Second of April" (l. 49); this kind of enumeration again can be traced to the times when ballads were recited and not read. This stylistic device can be found again in the next stanzas when we learn that Victor has to propose three times before Anna accepts him as her husband ("The first time ..." l. 53, "The second time ..." l. 55, "The third time ..." l. 61).

Again Victor is portrayed in a very unfavourable way. His future wife thinks he is "as dull as a wet afternoon" (l. 59), but she feels a need to settle down, so they get married in August. Whereas her kisses to the men she gives herself to are "like the best champagne" (l. 47) her kiss to Victor when she accepts his proposal is "like a blow on the head" (l. 63). Victor on the other hand compares her to "Helen of Troy", the most beautiful woman in Ancient Greece, who was a daughter of Zeus and the indirect cause of the Trojan War. She was also regarded a shallow woman without morals. However, Victor really calls Anna Helen because he admires her physical beauty.

Part Four:

In this part we find out that Victor has changed considerably since his marriage. He is happy and even wearing a flower in his buttonhole, a sign of the good state he is in. He does not even care that he is late for work although that would have been cause for anger for him before. In stanzas 19 and 20 when he learns that his colleagues had affairs with his wife the line "The door was just ajar" (ll. 74, 78) is repeated which underlines the fateful coincidence of Victor overhearing what his colleagues say. The shock he suffers is stressed by the alliteration in line 77 "stood still as a statue." It must seem especially cruel to Victor that one of his colleagues romped with his wife in a "Baby Austin car" (l. 80). This car is known for its smallness and so implies extreme closeness.

Part Five:

This part is quite typical of a ballad. There are a lot of repetitions especially in the beginnings of the stanzas ("Victor walked" l. 81, "Victor looked up" ll. 85 / 89, "Victor came" ll. 93, 97, 101). These lines also underline Victor's unhappiness and desperate search for help. Being a person without friends Victor does not turn to people but to the sky and nature with his despair ("sunset", "sky" ll. 85 / 87, "mountains" l. 89, "forest" l. 93, "meadow" l. 97, "river" l. 101). He asks them all for help, talking through them to his father. "Father" here could be his dead father or another name for God. He repeatedly calls on his father, always receiving the same answer, namely that his wife is an unworthy person who must die. Stanzas 22 to 26 show the same pattern: Victor turning to nature, asking his question addressing his father and receiving a negative answer. These repetitions also show that Victor is very desperate and has fallen into a frenzy over his wife's bad character.

Part Six:

After eight stanzas that have started with "Victor" the first stanza of part six starts with "Anna" and thus shifts the focus of the reader towards the victim of Victor's rage. Again there is a repetition: "Anna was sitting at table" (ll. 105 / 107) which underlines how peaceful and unsuspecting Anna is sitting at home waiting for Victor. Victor's crazy state of mind is reflected in stanza 31 where we find three repetitions of "There was a voice" (ll. 117–119) which shows that Victor hears voices that order him to kill her. Typically of Victor he admonishes her to prepare to meet God (l. 132). Anna's struggle is expressed by the parallel structure of stanzas 33 and 34. The first two lines of each start with Anna doing something to flee from Victor, however, she does not stand a chance against her wild husband.

Part Seven:

In the last three stanzas we see Victor after his murder. He still is convinced that what he did was the right thing. We can see that because of his quotations from the Bible. He quotes Jesus in each of the final stanzas. The contrast between "He" repeated in lines 137 and 138 and "They" in lines 141 and 142 stresses the gap between Victor and society. He has turned into a "lump of moss" (l. 143) by his deed and the fact that he is making a clay model of a woman in the last stanza expresses his disappointment with his wife.

Im Vergleich zu Marvells *To His Coy Mistress* sollte erwähnt werden, dass Auden alltägliche Sprache verwendet und dass sein Held keineswegs eine ganz besondere Person ist, sondern dass es sich bei Victor um einen ganz gewöhnlichen Menschen handelt, dessen Schicksal, das recht nüchtern geschildert wird, dennoch den Leser anrührt.

> Compare the two poems *To His Coy Mistress* and *Victor.* What are the differences in regard to language and style?

> Whereas Marvell writes about a very special person Auden describes a rather ordinary man. Marvell uses very poetic language, especially when he is describing his lady. Auden uses everyday language and does not employ unusual stylistic devices to tell his story of Victor. He uses direct speech and thus creates the impression of telling a story rather than of writing a poem.

Nach der Besprechung dieses langen Gedichtes sollen die Schülerinnen und Schüler nun einen kurzen Artikel für eine Zeitung über Victors Fall schreiben. Diese Aufgabe kann als Hausaufgabe die Bearbeitung des Gedichtes abschließen.

> Write a short article for a newspaper about Victor's case.

Nach dem Abschluss der Interpretation dieser beiden ziemlich langen Gedichte werden nun noch zwei kürzere Texte vorgestellt, die ebenfalls das Thema Liebe behandeln. Zunächst folgt ein Gedicht über das Ende einer Liebe, das passenderweise *Ending* heißt. Vor dem Lesen dieses Gedichtes sollen die Schülerinnen und Schüler Vermutungen darüber anstellen, was in einem Gedicht mit solch einem Titel beschrieben werden könnte. Vermutlich werden sie leicht auf die richtige Lösung kommen, das Ende einer Beziehung.

> The next poem we are going to read is called *Ending.* Do you have any ideas what this poem could be about?

Nun wird dieses Gedicht laut vorgetragen und soll kurz zusammengefasst werden. Danach werden die Schülerinnen und Schüler aufgefordert, in Partnerarbeit herauszuarbeiten, mit welchen sprachlichen Mitteln Gavin Ewart das Ende der Liebe darstellt. Die Ergebnisse dieser Untersuchung können in einem Tafelbild festgehalten werden.

> What is the poem *Ending* about?

> This poem is about the ending of a relationship or love affair. The poet describes how things have changed between two people.

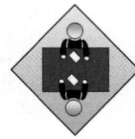

> How does Ewart describe the end of this relationship?

> Ewart contrasts the past with the present to describe the end of the relationship. He writes his poem in seven couplets, each describing the difference between then and now. Except for the first couplet the couplets rhyme a, a, b, b and so on. That is because the first couplet states that his love that was supposed to be eternal is now cooling off. The comparison with a "congealing chip" (l. 2) reminds the reader of something disgusting and rotting. In the following five couplets this comparison is worked out body part by body part.

Body parts	then	now
kiss (ll. 3/4)	hot as curry	in a hurry
hands (ll. 5/6)	electric charges	moored barges
feet (ll. 7/8)	ran to meet a date	running slow and late
eyes (ll. 9/10)	shone, seldom shut	power cut
parts (ll. 11/12)	transmitted joy	cold and coy

Notizen:

_____

_____

_____

_____

_____

_____

_____

_____

_____

_____

_____

_____

_____

_____

_____

_____

Gavin Ewart, *Ending*

The love we thought would never stop
now cools like a congealing chip.
The kisses that were hot as curry
are bird-pecks taken in a hurry.
5 The hands that held electric charges
now lie inert as four moored barges.
The feet that ran to meet a date
are running slow and running late.
The eyes that shone and seldom shut
10 are victims of a power cut.
The parts that then transmitted joy
are now reserved and cold and coy.
Romance, expected once to stay,
has left a note saying GONE AWAY.

congealing change from soft to solid

moored secured by anchor

Rupert Brooke, *Sonnet*

Hand trembling towards hand; the amazing lights
Of heart and eye. They stood on supreme heights.
Ah, the delirious weeks of honeymoon!
Soon they returned, and, after strange adventures,
5 Settled at Balham by the end of June.
Their money was in Can. Pacs. B. Debentures,
And in Antofagastas. Still he went
Cityward daily; still she did abide
At home. And both were really quite content
10 With work and social pleasures. Then they died.
They left three children (besides George, who drank):
The eldest, Jane, who married Mr Bell,
William, the head-clerk in the County Bank,
And Henry, a stock-broker, doing well.

Antofagastas seaport in Chile
abide remain, stay

The last couplet is funny although the theme of the poem is sad. Personified Romance has left this couple and left a note.

Describe the atmosphere that is created by Ewart in this poem.

In this poem the poet describes meticulously but without any expression of emotion the ending of his and his partner's love. The effect of this way of writing about something that is usually connected with a lot of feeling is that of detachment. It stresses the hopelessness of the situation, this couple will not find love again.

Dieses einfach aufgebaute Gedicht, das dennoch eine Atmosphäre erzeugt, kann als Grundlage für eigene Gedichte der Schülerinnen und Schüler dienen. Falls eigene Gedichte produziert und vorgetragen werden, sollte man die Klasse motivieren, solche Texte im Klassenzimmer auszuhängen oder in der Schülerzeitung zu veröffentlichen. Eine kreative Hausaufgabe motiviert den Kurs zur Arbeit an weiteren Gedichten.

Taking this poem as a pattern, try to write a poem contrasting now and then or here and there or you and someone else etc.

Nun wird das zweite kurze Gedicht gelesen. Man sollte den Titel *Sonnet* weglassen und die Schülerinnen und Schüler auffordern, selbst einen Titel für dieses Gedicht zu finden. Vermutlich werden dabei Titel genannt werden, die den Inhalt des Gedichtes zusammenfassen. Danach soll untersucht werden, um was für ein Gedicht es sich handelt. Aufgrund der in *Component* 1 gewonnenen Erkenntnisse sollte die Klasse auf die, wenn auch leicht abgewandelte, Form des Sonetts stoßen. Ein Tafelbild fasst die Ergebnisse der Analyse zusammen.

Can you give this poem a title?

- The meaning of life
- Marriage
- From marriage to the grave

Analyse the rhyme scheme and metrical pattern of this poem. In which way are there correspondences to the content?

Rhyme scheme: a, a,   b, c, b, c,   d, e, d, e,   f, g, f, g

Metrical pattern: iambic pentameter

This poem consists of 14 lines; it is a sonnet although the couplet that is expected at the end of the poem is at the beginning. The first two lines run on and rhyme so that they are set apart from the rest of the poem. This corresponds with their content. In those days the couple was very much in love and stood on "supreme heights" (l. 2). Line three is an exclamation describing the happiness of their honeymoon. From then on life has become more and more a routine that neither of them has ever questioned. They stick to the rules society dictates: the husband goes to work in the city, the wife remains at home in the suburbs; they have four children. One son no longer counts as their child as he is a drunkard and as such no longer accepts society's rules.

Viewed according to form there are three parts in this poem except for the opening couplet.

lines 3–6: honeymoon – adventures – settlement
lines 7–10: routine of work
lines 11–14: children

Dieses Gedicht schließt den Themenkomplex Liebe ab.

Notizen:

_____

_____

_____

_____

_____

_____

_____

_____

_____

_____

_____

_____

_____

_____

_____

_____

_____

_____

Component 3: War Poetry

In diesem *Component* werden fünf Gedichte aus dem Themenkreis Krieg vorgestellt. Während die ersten beiden Gedichte *The Volunteer* und *The General* aus dem Ersten Weltkrieg berichten, beziehen sich *In the Beginning was the Word* und *Picture from the Blitz* auf den Zweiten Weltkrieg. Das letzte Gedicht beschäftigt sich mit unterschiedlichen Kriegsschauplätzen und ist als Appell gegen das Vergessen zu verstehen.

Als Einstieg in das Thema kann man die Klasse auffordern, in Stichworten Szenen zu beschreiben, die in Kriegszeiten möglich sind. Dabei sollten nicht nur das Kriegsgeschehen selbst, sondern auch das Leben der in der Heimat zurückgebliebenen Angehörigen berücksichtigt werden. Beispielsweise könnte man die Gedanken eines Soldaten / einer Mutter / eines Kindes notieren oder zerstörte Städte / Häuser / Landschaften / Kriegsmaschinerie beschreiben lassen. Das Augenmerk der Klasse sollte besonders auf Adjektive gelenkt werden. Hierbei bietet sich eine Partnerarbeit an.

Think about situations that can occur in times of war. For example you could describe somebody's (a soldier's / a mother's / a child's ...) thoughts or a bombed / destroyed city / house / landscape. Take notes and think especially about adjectives that you could use.

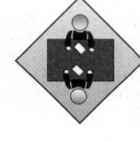

Im Anschluss an diese Aufgabe werden die Szenen vorgestellt und eventuell diskutiert.

Nun werden die Gedichte *The Volunteer* und *The General* (folgende Kopiervorlage) verteilt. Herbert Asquith's Gedicht wird einmal laut vorgetragen und dann in Gruppenarbeit analysiert. Die Information, dass das Gedicht aus dem Ersten Weltkrieg stammt, kann man vorab geben, oder man kann die Schülerinnen und Schüler im Anschluss an die Interpretation Vermutungen über den Entstehungszeitraum anstellen lassen.

What is the poem about?

This poem is about a clerk who goes to war and dies.

Analyse the rhyme scheme and metrical pattern of the poem.

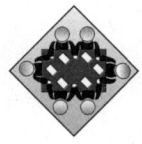

This poem consists mainly of iambic pentameters with two exceptions in lines 2 and 3 where the lines start with trochees. The rhyme scheme is fairly regular and consists of an embracing and a cross rhyme (a, b, b, a, c, d, c, d).

Herbert Asquith, *The Volunteer*

Here lies a clerk who half his life had spent
Toiling at ledgers in a city grey,
Thinking that so his days would drift away
With no lance broken in life's tournament.
5 Yet ever 'twixt the books and his bright eyes
The gleaming eagles of the legions came,
And horsemen, charging under phantom skies,
Went thundering past beneath the oriflamme.

And now those waiting dreams are satisfied;
10 From twilight to the halls of dawn he went;
His lance is broken; but he lies content
With that high hour, in which he lived and died.
And falling thus he wants no recompense,
Who found his battle in the last resort;
15 Nor need he any hearse to bear him hence,
Who goes to join the men of Agincourt.

ledgers books for book-keeping

oriflamme military flag

hearse vehicle used to carry corpses
Agincourt 14th century battle

Siegfried Sassoon, *The General*

"Good morning; good-morning!" the General said
When we met him last week on our way to the line.
Now the soldiers he smiled at are most of 'em dead,
And we're cursing his staff for incompetent swine.
5 "He's a cheery old card," grunted Harry to Jack
As they slogged up to Arras with rifle and pack.

Arras French town

But he did for them both by his plan of attack.

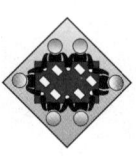

How is war described? What is the author's attitude towards war? Take the title of the poem into consideration.

In this poem war is clearly glorified. It is not realistically described with all its dangers and horrors, but it seems to be regarded as a means to uplift meaning of life. Right in the first line the reader learns that the clerk, the protagonist of this poem has died ("Here lies ..."). His life as a civilian is described in the first stanza.

The clerk lives in a "grey" (l. 2) city where he has quite a boring job "toiling at" (l. 2) books and waiting for his chance to break his lance in life's tournament (l. 4). This metaphor is taken from the medieval times of chivalry when brave knights fought for their countries and ladies. This image is referred to again in line 6, when the clerk dreams of metal and "gleaming" eagles that used to be carried in front of the army. He also dreams of horsemen galloping under visionary skies.

In the second stanza the reader finds out that the clerk's dream has become true and from the title of the poem it can be concluded that he enlisted as a volunteer. However, the word *die* is not used here, instead this, the author uses a euphemism "to the halls of dawn he went" (l. 10).

Even though the clerk has died the author speaks of his dreams being satisfied (l. 9). The fact that he is dead is referred to as his broken lance (l. 10) thus remaining in the image of chivalry and using again a euphemism. The author presumes that he lies in his grave as a content person and without any demand of retaliation. Again the contrast to civil life comes up when the hearse, a vehicle used when civilians die is refuted and also the image of medieval times appears once more when it is mentioned that he has joined "the men of Agincourt" (l. 16).

So one can say that the author glorifies war and thinks that dying for one's country is something one can be envied for.

Guess when this poem was written. Give reasons.

Answers will vary here depending on how well informed the students are about the patriotic surge in Great Britain during the time of the outbreak of World War I.

Nach der Besprechung dieses Gedichtes sollen die Schülerinnen und Schüler sich nun nochmals die Ergebnisse ihrer Gruppenarbeit vornehmen und vergleichen, welche Worte sie zur Beschreibung von Kriegsszenen gefunden haben und welche man in Asquith's Gedicht findet. Es wird bis auf das Wort *dead* vermutlich zu keinen Überschneidungen kommen.

Nach der Besprechung dieses Gedichtes sollte nun das zweite Gedicht als Hausaufgabe gelesen und kurz interpretiert werden. Die Hauptfrage bei der Lektüre sollte sich auf die Einstellung des Autors zum Krieg beziehen.

Read the poem *The General,* state what it is about and identify Siegfried Sassoon's attitude towards war.

This poem is about young soldiers who have to die because their leaders are incompetent.

Siegfried Sassoon has a more critical attitude towards war. In his poem he describes war as a truly terrifying experience in which many soldiers are killed. In his poem there is "cursing" (l. 4) because of bad leaders and instead of marching or charging soldiers "slog" (l. 6) along, an expression which reflects the hardship of walking for miles with "rifle and pack" (l. 6).

Nach der Besprechung der Hausaufgabe sollte man die beiden Gedichte in einem Gespräch vergleichen und die Ergebnisse in einem Tafelbild festhalten.

▮ Now let us compare these two poems.

The Volunteer	*The General*
two regular stanzas	5 plus 1 line
high register of language	colloquial language, slang used by soldiers
medieval ideals	Harry and Jack = ordinary people
Agincourt (ideal)	Arras (place of real battle)
glorification of military staff	critical attacks of military staff

Nach diesem Vergleich kann man den Schülerinnen und Schülern das nächste Gedicht vorlegen, diesmal ein Text, der sich mit dem Zweiten Weltkrieg auseinander setzt. Der Text *In the Beginning was the Word* wird verteilt und laut vorgetragen. Der Unterschied zu den beiden vorherigen Gedichten lässt sich schnell feststellen; es gibt kein regelmäßiges Reimschema und kein metrisches Muster.

▮ In which way does this poem vary from the other two poems we have read so far?

This poem deals with another war, namely World War II and it is a free verse poem. There is no real rhyme scheme, however, certain lines in the stanzas rhyme, as for instance lines 4 and 5 "failed" and "wailed".

Nach diesem Einstieg sollte die Struktur des Gedichtes untersucht werden. Es bietet sich wiederum eine Partnerarbeit an, jedoch ist diese Aufgabe auch als Hausaufgabe geeignet.

▮ Analyse the structure of the poem. What time span is described in the poem? What is said about the different stages described here?

This poem starts with the memories of a six-year-old and covers the time of World War II till the peace negotiations.

The first stanza is about the speaker when she is six years old telling her mother that she wishes for war. This wish is underlined by a recurring alliteration on "w": lines 1/2: When I was six I wanted war. Obsessed with words, ... and later in lines 5–7 again.

The second stanza deals with the time shortly after the outbreak of war. It is written mostly in iambic trimeters; there are rhymes in lines 1, 2 and 4 and lines 6 and 8. This stanza sounds hectic because of the short sentences and the short lines and so it reflects the hectic atmosphere at a time of war.
Stanza three describes how unreal peace seemed in the days of war. There is a rhyme in lines 2 and 4 and the rhythm is again a mixture of iambic trimeters and

Sheila Perry,
In the Beginning was the Word

When I was six I wanted war.
Obsessed with words,
I asked my mother to explain.
She tried, but failed,
5 "I wish there would be war", I wailed
And wondered at her anger
And why her face was pale.

The time was 1939,
There wasn't long to wait;
10 The world blamed Adolf Hitler
But I knew who called down fate,
My greed to taste the apple
From the forbidden tree.
It wasn't Hitler started the war,
15 I knew that it was me.

Peace was just another word,
Lost in myth and fable;
As strange and distant to us then
As Arthur and his table.
20 Still it eludes our feeble grasp
As the sword sinks in the lake.

We had a holiday for peace,
Not knowing it was fake.
A feast of parties in the street
25 When all the neighbours came.
But the Lord of the Dance
Had nails in His feet
And the great white bird was lame.

© Schöningh Verlag, Best.-Nr. 041227-4

tetrameters. Because of its references to mythical times it is fitting that the meter gives the impression of a ballad being recited.

In the last stanza peace has finally been restored, however, the speaker does not trust it, but calls it a fake.

Nach der Analyse der Strophen und der Struktur des Gedichtes sollte man nun die auffälligen Anspielungen in diesem Gedicht untersuchen. Dabei muss man den Titel mit einbeziehen.

In this poem there are many allusions. Identify and explain them. Take the title into consideration.

There are allusions to the Bible and to the old myth of King Arthur in this poem. The title is a quotation from the Bible (John, 1.1). It refers to the girl's wish for something she only knows the name of, something she does not know the meaning of. In the second stanza it is said that the speaker's "greed to taste the apple from the forbidden tree" started the war. This, of course, is an allusion to Eve seducing Adam in the Garden of Eden. In the last stanza there is an allusion to the crucification of Jesus – the Lord of the Dance's feet are nailed.

In the third stanza not the Bible is referred to but ancient myths. The legend of King Arthur and his round table come to mind when you read about "Arthur and his table" (l. 4) and that the sword (= Excalibur) disappears in the lake (l. 6). These allusions give the reader the impression that peace really did not seem possible at all. The biblical allusions reflect people's hope during the time of war. However, the last allusion to the Lord's nailed feet in combination with the title "Lord of the Dance", referring probably to the feasting neighbours stress the speaker's view that hope for real peace is quite futile.

The last line does not contain an allusion but rather a symbol – "the great white bird" could be a white dove, the world-wide symbol of peace. It is described as lame thus again underlining the speaker's belief that peace is a fake.

Nach diesem Gedicht, das die gesamte Kriegszeit beschreibt, folgt nun ein Gedicht, das nur eine einzige Szene aus diesem Krieg beschreibt und damit das Schreckliche der Kriegszeit exemplarisch und eindrücklich schildert.

Zunächst sollte das Gedicht laut vorgetragen werden. Danach kann die Frage gestellt werden, welch ein Unterschied zwischen diesem Gedicht und *In the Beginning was the Word* besteht. Wenn die Schülerinnen und Schüler erkannt haben, dass einmal eine längere Zeitspanne und hier eine Szene beschrieben werden, sollte die Frage angeschlossen werden, was für eine Situation in dem Gedicht beschrieben wird.

Beide Aufgaben können als Hausaufgabe zur Vorbereitung der weiteren Arbeit an diesem Gedicht gestellt oder in der Klasse in Einzelarbeit gelöst werden.

Notizen:

_____

_____

_____

_____

Lois Clark, *Picture from the Blitz*

After all these years
I can still close my eyes and see
her sitting there,
in her big armchair,
5 grotesque under an open sky,
framed by the jagged lines of her broken house.

Sitting there,
a plump homely person,
steel needles still in her work-rough hands;
10 grey with dust, stiff with shock,
but breathing,
no blood or distorted limbs;
breathing, but stiff with shock,
knitting unravelling on her apron'd knee.

15 They have taken the stretchers off my car
and I am running
under the pattering flack
over a mangled garden;
treading on something soft
20 and fighting the rising nausea –
only a far-flung cushion, bleeding feathers.

They lift her gently
out of her great armchair,
tenderly,
25 under the open sky,
a shock-frozen woman trailing khaki wool.
(Lois Clark)

mangled destroyed by twisting or tearing up

What is the difference between this poem and *In the Beginning was the Word*?

This poem does not describe the time between the outbreak of war and peace but only one scene from the time of the first bombing of England by the Germans.

Give a brief description of this scene.

In this poem Lois Clark describes a woman who has lost her home because of a bomb attack. Her house has obviously collapsed without hurting her; she is left sitting on her lawn in her armchair. She is in a state of shock. The speaker seems to be a doctor or ambulance driver because somebody gets a stretcher from her car.

Nachdem die Situation geklärt ist, sollten die Schülerinnen und Schüler genau die Beschreibung des Opfers untersuchen. Die Ergebnisse dieser Partnerarbeit können in einem Tafelbild festgehalten werden.

How is the woman described?

- sitting in an armchair (l. 3)
- grotesque (l. 5)
- plump homely person (l. 8)
- with work-rough hands (l. 9)
- grey (l. 10)
- stiff with shock (l. 10)
- wearing an apron (l. 14)
- shock-frozen woman (l. 26)

The woman appears to be a house-wife who is possibly knitting socks or a pullover for soldiers, since she is knitting with khaki wool. She has always worked hard, that is why her hands are so rough. She is wearing an apron, which shows that she was hit by the bomb attack while she was busy with her housework. The image created by these attributes does not fit to the woman who is "shock-frozen" by the bomb. Obviously she has not moved since the roof fell down, she is "grey with dust".

Nach der detaillierten Beschäftigung mit dieser Figur kann die Struktur des Gedichtes analysiert werden. Es empfiehlt sich wiederum eine Gruppenarbeit, da es für die Lerngruppe viel zu entdecken gibt.

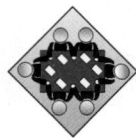

Analyse the structure of this poem and explain the stylistic devices used by Clark. Take the title into consideration.

The first stanza reveals that the speaker is thinking about this scene from the Blitzkrieg several years after the war. The poem is a description of what she sees when closing her eyes. Some phrases from this stanza are repeated later in the poem. For instance line 3 "sitting there" is repeated in line 7, the "big armchair" (l. 4) is repeated at the end of the poem in line 23 as "great armchair", the expression "under an open sky" (l. 5) is repeated in line 25 and so the poem comes to a full cycle.

The first two stanzas describe the victim of the attack. The word play "steel needles still" (l. 9) underlines the immobility of the woman. The elliptical sentence structure in combination with short expressions stresses the impression that a picture is being described. There is a parallelism in line 10 and a chiasm in lines 11 and 13 ("but breathing ... breathing, but") and the repetition of the phrase "stiff with shock" (ll. 10 and 14) underlines that effect. The contrast between her unmoving appearance and the fact that she does not appear to be injured is stressed by this word order.

The third stanza describes what the speaker did. The short lines stress the hectic atmosphere that has prevailed in this situation. The soft thing that the speaker has stepped on is just a cushion. However, her first fear that she may have trodden on a corpse or something of the kind fortunately has not come true. Instead, she employs the metaphor of the cushion "bleeding feathers", which (l. 21) has the effect of extreme violence in a poem that so far has dealt with the bomb attack without much use of words of the word field "violence".

The fourth stanza reports in few words how the woman is brought away. The contrast between the adverbs "gently" (l. 22) and "tenderly" (l. 24) that describe the movements of the helpers with the adjective "shock-frozen" (l. 26) that describes the state of the woman show how shocked not only the victim is but also those who come to her aide.

The title is connected with the poem in line 6 where it is said that the woman is "framed" by the remnants of her home. This word fits the expression "Picture" in the title.

Das letzte Gedicht in diesem *Component* ist Carl Sandburgs kurzes Gedicht *Grass*, das Schlachtfelder aus der Sicht des Grases reflektiert.

Das Gedicht wird wiederum vorgetragen. Eventuell müssen die geografischen Begriffe Austerlitz, Waterloo, Gettysburg, Ypres und Verdun erläutert werden. Dies kann als Hausaufgabe oder als Information den Schülerinnen und Schülern gegeben werden.

Explain the geographical names in this poem.
All of these places are places of battles:

Austerlitz	town in Czechoslovakia, today Slavkov; Battle of three Emperors, 2.12.1805, one of Napoleon's greatest victories, defeated Russian and Austrian
Waterloo	town near Brussels, Napoleon's final defeat, 18.6.1815
Gettysburg	near Harrisburg, PA, 1. – 3.7.1863, major battle in the American Civil War
Ypres	French town, three major battles of World War I, 1915 first use of poison gas by Germans, more than 250.000 Allied soldiers lost their lives there
Verdun	Feb. 21–July 1916, one of the most devastating engagements of World War I

Carl Sandburg, *Grass*

Pile the bodies high at Austerlitz and Waterloo.
Shovel them under and let me work –
I am the grass; I cover all.

And pile them high at Gettysburg
5 And pile them high at Ypres and Verdun.
Shovel them under and let me work.
Two years, ten years, and passengers ask the conductor:
What place is this?
Where are we now?

10 I am the grass.
Let me work.

Nach der Erläuterung der geografischen Namen kann man sich dem Inhalt des Textes zuwenden. Zunächst sollte geklärt werden, wer der Sprecher dieses Gedichtes ist und weshalb Carl Sandburg diese ungewöhnliche Perspektive eingenommen hat.

Who is the speaker of the poem? Why do you think Sandburg chose this point of view?

The speaker of the poem is grass which is quite unusual. Maybe Sandburg wants to demonstrate how meaningless wars and deaths of soldiers are when looked upon through the eyes of nature. The grass stands for the forces of nature that are much more powerful than human beings because they can cover everything human beings do and can render it invisible.

Da offensichtlich die Nutzlosigkeit von Kriegen angeprangert wird, kann eine kurze stilistische Analyse verdeutlichen, wie Sandburg seine Auffassung von Krieg dem Leser nahe bringt.

What stylistic devices does Carl Sandburg employ to demonstrate the futility of war?

We find a repetition of the expressions "pile them" (ll. 1, 4, 5), "let me work" (ll. 2 and 10) which stress the stubborness of nature. Also the phrase "I am the grass" (ll. 3 and 9) underlines the determination of the grass to make human atrocities disappear.
Except for these repetitions there is a climax in line 7: "Two years, ten years ...", which also shows that war is futile because after a rather short time, after the grass has done its work, people do not even remember what has happened there.

Nach der Erarbeitung dieses Gedichtes kann man sich einem neuen Themenkomplex in einem weiteren *Component* zuwenden.

Notizen:

_____

_____

_____

_____

_____

_____

_____

_____

_____

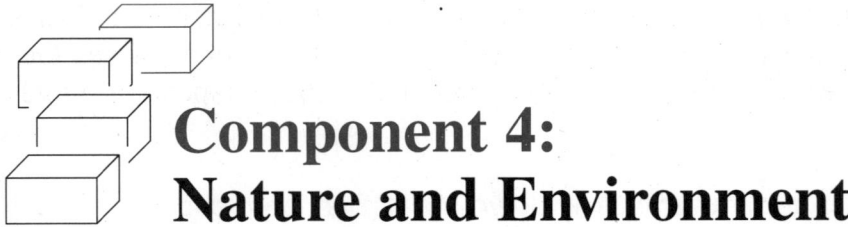

Component 4:
Nature and Environment

In diesem *Component* werden fünf Gedichte und ein Songtext vorgestellt, deren Thema die Naturbetrachtung ist. Dabei gehören drei Gedichte eng zusammen. Wordsworth's *The Daffodils* gehört zu einem der berühmtesten Gedichte der englischsprachigen Literatur. Dies lässt sich auch daran erkennen, dass es mehrfach von Dichtern in späterer Zeit wieder aufgenommen worden ist, so beispielsweise von Lynn Peters, die es unter einem feministischen Gesichtspunkt rezipiert, und Adrian Henri, der es nutzt, um den Kontrast zwischen Natur und Technik in unserer Zeit darzustellen.

Jeni Conzyn's Gedicht *Complaint of the Water* verfolgt den Lauf eines fließenden Wassers ins Meer aus der Sicht des Wassers. Der letzte Text dieses *Component* ist ein Songtext von den Talking Heads, der beschreibt, was passiert, wenn der Traum der Naturliebhaber wahr wird und unsere Umgebung tatsächlich in den Zustand unberührter Natur zurückgeführt wird.

Einstieg in das Thema bietet das Gedicht *The Tiger* von William Blake, in dem durch die Betrachtung eines Tigers über die Natur Gottes nachgedacht wird.

Zu Beginn sollte man den Schülerinnen und Schülern lediglich den Titel des Gedichtes nennen und sie dann auffordern zu spekulieren, wie ein solches Gedicht aussehen könnte, das einen Tiger zum Thema hat. Die von der Klasse genannten Begriffe können in einem Tafelbild festgehalten werden.

The poem we are going to read now is called *The Tiger*. Can you imagine what it is about and how a tiger could be described?

> - yellow, orange, black
> - dangerous
> - man-eater
> - living in a zoo / in the jungle
> - huge claws / teeth / body

Anschließend wird das Gedicht verteilt und laut vorgetragen. Im Vergleich zu ihren eigenen Begriffen sollte die Klasse nun erläutern, wie Blake den Tiger beschreibt. Wo sind Übereinstimmungen, wo Abweichungen? Für diese Aufgabe eignet sich eine Partnerarbeit.

Compare the poem to your ideas about how to describe a tiger naming differences and similarities.

The bright colours of the tiger could be meant by the expression "burning bright" (ll. 1 and 21). The fact that the tiger is a very dangerous animal is expressed in various phrases, e. g. "thy fearful symmetry" (ll. 4 and 24), the questions

William Blake, *The Tiger*

Tiger! Tiger! burning bright
In the forest of the night,
What immortal hand or eye
Could frame thy fearful symmetry?

5 In what distant deeps or skies
Burnt the fire of thine eyes?
On what wings dare he aspire?
What the hand dare seize the fire?

And what shoulder, and what art,
10 Could twist the sinews of thy heart?
And when thy heart began to beat,
What dread hand, and what dread feet?

What the hammer? What the chain?
In what furnace was thy brain?
15 What the anvil? What dread grasp
Dare its deadly terrors clasp?

When the stars threw down their spears,
And watered heaven with their tears,
Did he smile his work to see?
20 Did he who made the lamb make thee?

Tiger! Tiger! burning bright
In the forest of the night,
What immortal hand or eye
Dare frame thy fearful symmetry.

aspire rise up
what the hand which hand

shoulder refers to physical strength
art refers to spiritual inventiveness
sinews strong cord in body connecting muscle to bone

furnace container heated to high temperature for burning things
its refers to the brain

of how the tiger was created with "hammer" and "chain" (l. 13), that his brain was made in a "furnace" (l. 14) and with the help of an "anvil" (l. 15). Again, "deadly terrors" (l. 15) are associated with the tiger. This tiger does not live in a zoo, but in a "forest" (ll. 2 and 22) which could well be read as a jungle.

Nach dieser ersten Auseinandersetzung mit dem Gedicht sollte man die Schülerinnen und Schüler auffordern, darüber nachzudenken, ob Blake hier wirklich nur einen Tiger beschreibt oder ob er eine andere Absicht mit diesem Gedicht verfolgt. Welche Mittel benutzt er, um von der Ebene der Beschreibung eines Tigers zu seiner Intention, der Reflexion über den Akt der Schöpfung, überzuleiten? Diese Aufgabe eignet sich gut als Hausaufgabe. Die Ergebnisse sollten dann in einem Tafelbild festgehalten werden.

William Blake does not only describe a tiger in his poem. What is the author's real intention and what stylistic devices does he use to make his point?

The poem *The tiger* is only at first glance a poem about a tiger. It really deals with the question about the nature of God or a creator who has made an animal as fierce as a tiger. Blake's search for this creator is reflected in the numerous questions he asks. In the first five stanzas of the poem there are 11 questions about the process of creating a tiger. Obviously Blake imagines this process to have been quite violent since he uses so many words connected with a smith's workshop. In addition to that, there are a number of words from the word field "anatomy"; oddly though, the bodyparts named by Blake are not especially typical of a tiger. In the fifth stanza he asks himself the question that seems to puzzle him most, namely if the same creator could have created a tiger and a lamb, its complete opposite, at the same time. The contrast between the tiger and the lamb is underlined by the contrast between the fierce appearance of the tiger and the question if the creator has smiled upon his terrible work (l. 19). All in all, this poem expresses admiration of God's (= the creator's) ability to create fierce and cruel things like the tiger as well as good and peaceful beings as the lamb.

11 questions:	What immortal hand ...?	(ll. 3/4)
	In what distance ...?	(ll. 5/6)
	On what wings ...?	(l. 7)
	What the hand ...?	(l. 8)
	And what shoulder ...?	(ll. 9/10)
	And when thy hand ...?	(ll. 11/12)
	What the hammer?	(l. 13)
	What the chain?	(l. 13)
	In what furnace ...?	(l. 14)
	What the anvil?	(l. 15)
	What dread grasp ...?	(ll. 15/16)
	Did he smile ...?	(l. 19)
	Did he who made ...?	(l. 20)

words from word field "smith":

burning (fire)	(ll. 1/6/8/21)
hammer	(l. 13)
furnace	(l. 14)
anvil	(l. 15)

words from the word field "anatomy":

hand or eye	(ll. 3/23)
eyes	(l. 6)
hand	(l. 8)
shoulder	(l. 9)
sinews of thy heart	(l. 10)
heart	(l. 11)
hand / feet	(l. 12)
brain	(l. 14)

contrasts:	fire / forest (ll. 1/2; 21/22) – stars / tears / watered (ll. 17 / 18)
	tiger – lamb (l. 20)

Can you think of a reason why Blake used all these questions? Why did he structure the poem in this particular way?

When listening to this poem you get the impression that the hammering of the eleven questions reflects the hammering of the smith who works on creating the tiger.
The chant-like intonation of the first and last stanza stresses that the speaker seems to have fallen into a trance-like state while futilely pondering these questions.

Nach der Erarbeitung dieses eher düsteren und schwer verständlichen Gedichtes wird der Klasse das Gedicht *The Daffodils* von William Wordsworth vorgelegt. Die Besprechung dieses romantischen Gedichts, das die Natur als eine Quelle der Erholung und Ablenkung beschreibt, wird den Schülerinnen und Schülern leichter fallen. Zunächst sollte geklärt werden, was *daffodils* sind (Osterglocken), danach kann das Gedicht verteilt und laut vorgetragen werden.
Die Frage nach dem Inhalt lässt sich leicht beantworten. Falls die Schülerinnen und Schüler Vorwissen zum Thema Romantik haben, kann es hier mit eingebracht werden, falls nicht, sollte man lediglich untersuchen lassen, welches Verhältnis zur Natur das lyrische Ich in diesem Gedicht hat.

What is this poem about?

This poem is about the speaker taking a walk near a lake and discovering a host of daffodils which seems to strike him as an especially beautiful natural scene. He takes that image with him and finds happiness when remembering it at home in quiet moments.

William Wordsworth, *The Daffodils*

I wandered lonely as a cloud
That floats on high o'er vales and hills,
When all at once I saw a crowd,
A host, of golden daffodils;
5 Beside the lake, beneath the trees,
Fluttering and dancing in the breeze.

Continuous as the stars that shine
And twinkle on the Milky Way,
They stretched in never-ending line
10 Along the margin of a bay:
Ten thousand saw I at a glance,
Tossing their heads in sprightly dance.

The waves beside them danced; but they
Outdid the sparkling waves in glee:
15 A poet could not but be gay,   **gay** happy
In such a jocund company.   **jocund** cheerful, glad
I gazed, and gazed, but little thought
What wealth the show to me had brought;

For oft, when on my couch I lie
20 In vacant or in pensive mood,
They flash upon that inward eye
Which is bliss of solitude;
And then my heart with pleasure fills,
And dances with the daffodils.

© Schöningh Verlag, Best.-Nr. 041227-4

In Partnerarbeit sollen die Schülerinnen und Schüler nun erarbeiten, welche Vergleiche Wordsworth zieht, um die Schönheit der Osterglocken zu preisen. Ebenso sollen sie herausfinden, welches Wort mehrfach in Verbindung mit den Osterglocken genannt wird, und seine Wirkung erläutern. Die Ergebnisse dieser Partnerarbeit können kurz an der Tafel festgehalten werden.

What comparisons does Wordsworth make to show the beauty of the daffodils? Which word is repeated throughout the poem and why?

The daffodils are compared to the stars in the sky and to the water of the lake. The word repeated several times is "dance" (ll. 6, 12, 13, 24), describing the swift movements of the flowers in the wind. In the last stanza the speaker says that his heart dances with the daffodils, meaning that he is elevated and happy when he thinks about the beautiful image of the flowers near the lake.

Comparison: stars	lines 7/8	the flowers are as uncountable as the stars of the Milky Way
waves	lines 13/14	the flowers are sparkling more than the waters of the lake

Eine Untersuchung des Metrums zeigt, dass Wordsworth in jambischen Tetrametern schreibt, das Reimschema ist sehr gleichmäßig; jedoch gibt es drei metrische Abweichungen, die von der Klasse untersucht werden sollten. Es empfiehlt sich die Anfertigung einer Overheadfolie, um die Ergebnisse der metrischen Analyse dort eintragen zu können.

Analyse the rhyme scheme and metrical pattern of this poem.

This poem consists of four stanzas of six lines each with a regular rhyme scheme a, b, a, b, c, c. The metrical pattern consists of iambic tetrameters, however, there are three exceptions: first in the first stanza in line 6 where the line starts with a trochee instead of a iamb. The same happens in line 12 in the second stanza. In the first stanza the irregularity stresses the surprise of the speaker on looking upon the "fluttering" mass of flowers. In the second stanza the same image of moving flowers is stressed by the trochee "tossing". The last irregularity can be found in line 22 where an anapest "which is bliss" emphasises the speaker's happiness when recreating the image of the daffodils in his inward eye.

Im folgenden Gedicht nimmt die Autorin Lynn Peters Wordsworths Gedicht auf und spielt auf das Zusammenleben von William und seiner Schwester Dorothy an, die ihm den Haushalt führte und laut Peters ebenfalls dichterische Ambitionen hatte, die sie aber aufgrund der Tatsache, dass ihr die Hausarbeit überlassen blieb, nicht so ausleben konnte wie ihr Bruder. Die Schülerinnen und Schüler sollten zunächst die Verse nennen, die direkte Zitate aus Wordsworths Gedicht sind.

Dabei empfiehlt sich wiederum die Herstellung einer Overhead-Folie.

Lynn Peters, *Why Dorothy Wordsworth is not as Famous as her Brother*

"I wandered lonely as a ...
They're in the top drawer, William,
Under your socks –
I wandered lonely as a –
5 No not that drawer, the top one.
I wandered by myself –
Well wear the ones you can find,
No, don't get overwrought my dear,
I'm coming."

10 "I was out one day wandering
Lonely as a cloud when –
Softboiled egg, yes my dear,
As usual, three minutes –
As a cloud when all of a sudden –
15 Look, I said I'll cook it,
Just hold on will you –
All right. I'm coming."

"One day I was out for a walk
When I saw this flock –
20 It can't be too hard, it had three minutes.
Well put some butter in it.
This host of golden daffodils
As I was out for a stroll one –"

"Oh you fancy a stroll, do you.
25 Yes, all right William. I'm coming.
It's on the peg. Under your hat.
I'll bring my pad, shall I, in case
You want to jot something down?"

You can recognise certain quotations from William Wordsworth's poem *The Daffodils*. Identify those quotations and describe for which purpose Lynn Peters uses them.

In this poem you can find 10 verses in which the author quotes from *The Daffodils* or plays on quotes from this poem:

line 1:	I wandered lonely as a ...	this is the exact quote
line 4:	repeated	
line 6:	I wandered by myself	

Here you can see that the beginning of the poem has been twisted because of the repeated interruptions

lines 10/11:	I was out one day wandering
	Lonely as a cloud when –
line 14:	As a cloud when all of a sudden –
lines 18/19:	One day I was out for a walk
	When I saw this flock –
lines 22/23:	– This host of golden daffodils
	As I was out for a stroll one –

Lynn Peters uses these quotations and twisted lines from Wordsworth's poem to demonstrate how impossible it is for someone who is constantly interrupted by questions and demands referring to household-chores to write a poem. The speaker is Dorothy Wordsworth, the famous poet's sister. Dorothy is constantly interrupted by her brother, who cannot find the right article of clothing, asks for a soft-boiled egg, complains that his egg is not soft enough and who wants to go for a walk. The speaker's reaction to these interruptions show admiration for her brother and an admirable lack of irritation. She comes to his help (stanza one), obviously boils his egg (stanzas two / three), does not seem to mind the complaints and is ready to leave her writing in order to accompany her brother for a stroll and even offers to take a pad to enable him "to jot something down" (l. 28).

Obwohl in diesem Gedicht kein Reimschema zu erkennen ist, entsteht ein gewisser Rhythmus durch den Wechsel von Zitaten und Zurufen an den Bruder.

Falls die Schülerinnen und Schüler Interesse an dem Thema Frauen und Kunst zeigen, dürfte sich hier eine Diskussion über künstlerische Produktivität von Frauen anschließen.

Notizen:

_____

_____

_____

_____

_____

Adrian Henri, *The New, Fast, Automatic Daffodils**

(New variation on Wordsworth's "Daffodils")

I wandered lonely as
THE NEW, FAST DAFFODIL
     FULLY AUTOMATIC
that floats on high o'er vales and hills
5 The Daffodil is generously dimensioned to accommodate four adult passengers
10.000 saw I at a glance
Nodding their new anatomically shaped heads in sprightly dance
Beside the lake beneath the trees
     in three bright modern colours
10 red, blue and pigskin
The Daffodil de luxe is equipped with a host of useful accessoires
including windscreen wiper and washer with joint control
A Daffodil doubles the enjoyment of touring at home or abroad
in vacant or in pensive mood
15 SPECIFICATION:
     Overall width: 1 44 m (57")
     Overall height   1 38 m (54.3")
     Max. speed   105 km / hr (65 m.p.h.)
       (also cruising speed)
20 DAFFODIL
     RELIABLE – ECONOMICAL
DAFFODIL
     THE BLISS OF SOLITUDE
DAFFODIL
25   The Variomatic Inward Eye
Travelling by Daffodil you can relax and enjoy every mile of the journey.

* (Cut-up of Wordsworth's poem plus Dutch motor-car leaflet)

In dem dritten Gedicht, das sich mit einer Weiterführung von Wordsworths *Daffodils* beschäftigt, finden sich exakte Zitate aus diesem Gedicht und aus einer Werbung für ein Auto. Auch hier empfiehlt es sich, eine Folie von dem Gedicht herzustellen, um mit unterschiedlichen farbigen Folienschreibern diese beiden Textsorten zu markieren. Danach stellt sich die Frage, welchen Effekt diese Mischung der beiden Texte hat.

Mithilfe der Kopiervorlage von Wordsworths *Daffodils* können die Schülerinnen und Schüler leicht die Passagen in Henris Gedicht markieren, die direkt übernommen wurden. Diese Markierungen sollten dann auf die Folie übertragen und per Overhead-Projektor allen sichtbar gemacht werden. Nun stellt sich die Frage nach dem Effekt. Dafür bietet es sich an, in einer Gruppenarbeit die Schülerinnen und Schüler Beispiele dafür heraussuchen zu lassen, wie der Werbetexter sein Produkt anpreist.

Having identified the parts of the poem that originate from the *Daffodils* explain now how the advertiser praises his product, a car.

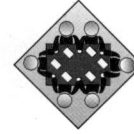

New, Fast, Automatic (l. 2) Fully Automatic (l. 3)	car of high technical standard
generously dimensioned (l. 5)	a lot of space, comfortable
three bright modern colours (l. 10)	attracts attention
Daffodil de luxe (l. 12)	luxury car
Daffodil doubles the enjoyment (l. 14)	promise of satisfaction
technical facts (ll. 16–20)	proves how good car is
you can relax and enjoy (l. 27)	enjoyment whenever you drive

Auf der Basis dieser Gruppenarbeit kann man nun im Gespräch den Effekt dieser Mischung der beiden Texte besprechen. Dabei sollte die Klasse herausarbeiten, dass jeweils das lyrische Ich der Gedichte auf der Suche nach Glück ist und zu ganz unterschiedlichen Glücksmomenten findet.

What is the effect of the juxtaposition of a Romantic poem with a modern car advertisement? Especially take into consideration who the speakers of the poems are.

By juxtaposing these two texts Henri achieves the effect that the modern reader recognises the old poem and realises that the search for happiness for today's readers has a different aim than for a reader about 200 years ago. Whereas the speaker in Wordsworth's poem finds bliss and happiness in solitude and the memory of a beautiful visual experience in nature, the speaker in Henri's poem refers to the enjoyment of driving a very comfortable, fast, fully automatic car which enables him or her to compare the experience of driving with 10.000 other drivers.

Wenn die Schülergruppe an dem Thema Technik und Natur interessiert ist, kann man als Hausaufgabe einen Kommentar zum Thema „Technik – menschliches Wunderwerk oder verdammenswerte Zerstörerin von Natur?" schreiben lassen.

Write a comment on the topic: Technical development – proof of supremacy of the human mind or hateful destroyer of natural resources?

Das nächste Gedicht ist interessant, weil es ein ungewöhnliches lyrisches Ich hat: Das Wasser spricht und klagt über die verschiedenen Einschränkungen, denen es ausgesetzt ist. Das Gedicht muss gründlich gelesen werden, da es sich beim ersten Lesen nicht sofort erschließen lässt.

Als Einstieg in die Arbeit mit diesem Gedicht bietet sich eine *pre-reading*-Aufgabe an. Der Titel des Gedichtes *Complaint of the Water* wird den Schülerinnen und Schülern genannt. Dann soll überlegt werden, worüber sich das Wasser beschweren könnte. Die Lerngruppe soll sich in Partnerarbeit zu dieser Fragestellung Notizen machen.

The title of our next poem is *Complaint of the Water.* Think of possible complaints the water could have and take notes.

- chemical waste in rivers, lakes, and oceans
- canals that determine where the water runs
- the sun in hot countries
- river control (e. g. the river Rhine)
- wasting water in households

Nach der Sammlung dieser und weiterer möglicher Beschwerden, die das Wasser an uns richten könnte, wird das Gedicht verteilt und einmal laut vorgetragen.
Das Gedicht ist sprachlich nicht einfach, daher empfiehlt es sich, den Schülerinnen und Schülern in einer Partnerarbeit die Aufgabe zu stellen, die tatsächlichen Beschwerden in diesem Gedicht herauszuarbeiten.

Read Jeni Couzyn's poem carefully and find out what complaints the water has in this poem.

- water is confused by man-made drains (l. 1)
- these drains hinder its progress (ll. 2/3)
- the passage through dark tubes prevents it from entering the open seas (ll. 4–10)
- plants drink it and turn it into material for their leaves (ll. 16–21)

Nach dieser inhaltlichen Klärung des Textes kann man sich der Untersuchung der Struktur und der stilistischen Analyse zuwenden. Dabei stellt sich die Frage nach dem lyrischen Ich; es sollte auf jeden Fall erwähnt werden, dass es sich um ein Gedicht in *free verse* handelt.

Jeni Couzyn, *Complaint of the Water*

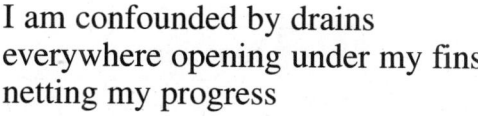

I am confounded by drains
everywhere opening under my fins
netting my progress

fins thin vertical part sticking out of a fish, which helps balance

labyrinths of stinking darkness
5 I am confounded by the rush of myself
everywhere the down-pull

hurl of me and sinking
my gross weight and hopeless
onrush of longing to

10 lose myself in the sea.
All that I love flee from: air
that opens its wings, mountains

and rock, and all that is steadfast
I knot myself against, fling myself
15 out and away from. All things

steadfast not changing quickly

eat me: veins and capillaries
suck me from my chosen
adventures and fasten me into

usurping flat flowers and leaves.
20 O you false blossoming dryness
that I must creep through unseen

and humbly, one day I shall
drown the world – all things will live
and swim in me.

© Schöningh Verlag, Best.-Nr. 041227-4

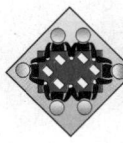

Read this poem again and analyse its point of view and the stylistic devices that are used. Take notes naming the devices and explain their function:

The point of view is interesting in this poem. The water itself is speaking to the reader. The author uses different stylistic devices to demonstrate how frustrated the water is about its current situation:

device	quotation	function
anaphora	I am confounded (ll. 1 + 5)	this anaphora stresses the water's confusion
metaphors	labyrinths of stinking darkness (l. 4)	the water's discontent is underlined
	air that opens its wings (ll. 11/12)	in contrast to the caught and hopeless water the air can escape
	false blossoming dryness (l. 20)	this dryness is false because nobody knows that water has been sucked up to feed the blossoms
contrast	water – air – rock (ll. 10–13)	this contrast shows how unhappy the water is compared to the other elements
parallelism	all things eat me ... suck me ... fasten me ... (ll. 15–18)	this parallel enumeration of what happens to the water because of earth and plants stresses its dependence
alliteration	flat flowers and leaves (l. 19)	the contempt for the falsely blossoming plants is shown

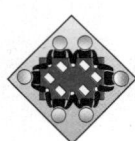

Analyse the meter, rhyme scheme and structure of this poem.

Since this poem is written in free verse it is impossible to detect any rhyme scheme or metrical pattern. However, each stanza consists of three lines. The sentences of this poem run on through several verses and so there are numerous enjambements.
At the end of the poem the water threatens the rest of the world and predicts that it will eventually drown everything. This threat is underlined by the contrast of the words "humbly" (l. 22) and the following sentence "one day I shall drown the world" (ll. 22/23).

Nach der Bearbeitung dieses Gedichtes kommt als letzter Text in diesem *Component* ein Liedtext der Talking Heads zur Sprache (aus: Naked, 1996, EMI). Falls man den Song auf Tonträger hat, sollte man ihn auf jeden Fall vorspielen und die Schülerinnen und Schüler auffordern zu versuchen, möglichst viel an Text zu verstehen. Wie bei vielen Gedichten kann man den Einstieg über den Titel des Songs suchen; die Antworten können verschiedenartig ausfallen.

The title of a songtext by The Talking Heads is *(Nothing but) Flowers.* Can you imagine what this text is about?

- The speaker of the text only wants to have flowers or give them to his beloved as a gift.
- The speaker does not like anything else but flowers.
- The text is about an old person who has nothing left in the world but a garden or balcony.
- This text describes a landscape where there are no buildings or man-made things but only natural elements like flowers.

Im Anschluss an diese Spekulationen wird der Text gehört bzw. gemeinsam gelesen. Zunächst kann man danach fragen, wovon allgemein dieser Text handelt, wer spricht und wann die Handlung des Textes spielen könnte.

Having listened to the text state what it is about, who is speaking and when the story takes place.

The speaker of the text is a person who finds himself in a landscape without any of the things that make up civilisation. The only things that he sees are flowers, fields and mountains. Cars, shopping malls and highways have disappeared. Obviously, this story takes place some time in the future when for reasons unknown the last vestiges of civilisation have disappeared.

Nach diesem Gespräch über den Inhalt des Liedtextes sollte man in einer Partnerarbeit darauf zu sprechen kommen, inwiefern man diesem Text anmerkt, dass es sich um ein Lied handelt, und wo die Gemeinsamkeiten zu den bisher gelesenen Gedichten liegen. Die Ergebnisse dieser Arbeit können in einem Tafelbild festgehalten werden.

Is this text a songtext or a poem? Why? Also find out where there are similarities between this text and the poems you have read so far.

Differences	Similarities
• there is a kind of refrain "You got it" after a parallel sentence structure • the lines are of similar length	• stylistic devices can be found as in the poems

Im Anschluss an die Ergebnissicherung sollten die verwendeten Stilmittel genauer untersucht werden.

The Talking Heads, *(Nothing but) Flowers*

Here we stand
Like an Adam and an Eve
Waterfalls
The Garden of Eden

5 **Two fools in love**
So beautiful and strong
The birds in the trees
Are smiling upon them
From the age of the dinosaur
10 Cars have run on gasoline
Where, where have they gone?
Now it's nothing but flowers

This used to be real estate
Now it's only fields and trees
15 Where, where is the town
Now, it's nothing but flowers
The highways and cars
Were sacrificed for agriculture
I thought that we'd start over
20 But I guess I was wrong
Once there were parking lots
Now it's a peaceful oasis
YOU GOT IT, YOU GOT IT
I miss the honky tonks,
25 Dairy Queens and 7–Elevens
YOU GOT IT, YOU GOT IT
And as things fell apart
Nobody paid much attention
YOU GOT IT, YOU GOT IT

30 There was a factory
Now there are mountains and rivers
YOU GOT IT, YOU GOT IT
We caught a rattlesnake
Now we got something for dinner
35 WE GOT IT, WE GOT IT
There was a shopping mall
Now it's all covered with flowers
YOU'VE GOT IT, YOU'VE GOT IT
If this is paradise
40 I wish I had a lawnmower
YOU'VE GOT IT, WE'VE GOT IT
Years ago
I was an angry young man
I'd pretend
45 That I was a billboard
Standing tall
By the side of the road
I fell in love
With a beautiful highway

50 I dream of cherry pies,
Candy bars and chocolate chip cookies
YOU GOT IT, YOU GOT IT
We used to microwave,
Now we just eat nuts and berries
55 YOU GOT IT, YOU GOT IT
This was a discount store,
Now it's turned into a cornfield
YOU GOT IT, YOU GOT IT
Don't leave me stranded here,
60 I can't get used to this lifestyle

(The Talking Heads, from: Naked, 1966, © EMI)

© Schöningh Verlag, Best.-Nr. 041227-4

What stylistic devices are employed and what is their effect?

Numerous stylistic devices are used in this text as in the poems before. The author uses **allusions** to the Bible, as in the first part "Adam" and "Eve" and "Garden of Eden", which evoke an image of paradise. A reference is made to the time of the dinosaurs to stress how long people have driven around in gasoline fuelled cars. The **anaphora** "where, where" (ll. 11, 15) underlines the speaker's longing for old amenities that people could enjoy. His disappointment is made clear by the **repetition** "Now it's nothing but flowers" (ll. 12, 16).

In addition to that the **contrasting** of phrases throughout the text stresses the abyss between life before and now:

"real estate" (l. 13)	"fields and trees" (l. 14)
"highways and cars" (l. 17)	"agriculture" (l. 18)
"parking lots" (l. 21)	"peaceful oasis" (l. 22)
"factory" (l. 30)	"mountains and rivers" (l. 31)
"shopping mall" (l. 36)	"all covered with flowers" (l. 37)
"microwave" (l. 53)	"nuts and berries" (l. 54)
"discount store" (l. 56)	"cornfield" (l. 57)

There is another instance where the new life referred to in the song is rejected. The speaker wishes for a lawnmower in order to get rid of all that paradise (ll. 39/40). Of course, this wish cannot be fulfilled because there will be no more lawnmowers.

Im Anschluss an die Besprechung dieses Textes kann man die Schülerinnen und Schüler danach fragen, auf welche der angesprochenen zivilisatorischen Errungenschaften sie gut oder nicht verzichten können. Daraufhin kann es zu einer Diskussion darüber kommen, wie das Leben ohne Autos und Konsumtempel aussehen würde und ob man selbst auch zu dem Schluss käme: *"I can't get used to this lifestyle."*
Hieran lässt sich die Hausaufgabe anschließen, einen zusammenfassenden Kommentar zu dem Thema zu verfassen.

Discuss what life without the everyday conveniences like cars, refrigerators, etc. would be like and if you would like to live in such a new world.

Anschließend kann zum nächsten *Component* übergegangen werden, in dem eher kreativ gearbeitet werden soll.

Notizen:

_____

_____

_____

_____

_____

_____

Component 5: Creative Approach

In diesem *Component* sollen Anregungen dazu gegeben werden, wie man die Schülerinnen und Schüler dazu bewegen kann, selber Gedichte zu schreiben. Als Einstieg in diese Arbeit kann man recht einfache, aber motivierende Aufgabenstellungen wählen. Man sollte mit dem Kurs ein Thema absprechen, über das gerne geschrieben wird. Es ist ratsam, allgemein gefasste Themen zu wählen wie Freundschaft, Liebe, Hass, Schule, Tiere usw. Dann werden verschiedene Möglichkeiten, diese Themen in kleine Gedichte zu fassen, vorgestellt, diese finden sich auf dem *Worksheet*. Als Beispiel wurde hier „Schule" gewählt. Die Schülerinnen und Schüler sollten hierbei nicht gemeinsam arbeiten, sondern jeder sollte versuchen, für sich eine Lösung zu finden. Auch sollte es dem Kurs freigestellt bleiben, die Ideen aufzugreifen und auf eigenen Blättern umzusetzen, die später in der Klasse aufgehängt werden können.

On your worksheet you will find different ideas about how you could approach the topic "school" when writing a poem. Please fill in the gaps and finish the poems.

Die verschiedenen Ergebnisse werden im Anschluss an die Einzelarbeit gemeinsam vorgestellt und besprochen. Dabei wird sich zeigen, dass einige „Autoren" nicht gerne ihre Arbeiten öffentlich präsentieren. Um nicht die Motivation für weitere Übungen einzudämmen, sollte man diese Scheu respektieren und nicht auf einer Vorstellung insistieren.

Nach diesen einstimmenden Übungen sollte man mit den *Shape Poems* fortfahren, da diese sprachlich vielseitige Möglichkeiten eröffnen. Dabei wird zunächst das Beispiel *poem about the sun slinking off and pinning up a notice* von Roger McGough vorgestellt und gemeinsam gelesen. Die Klasse soll Stellung zu diesem Gedicht nehmen und dann eigene *Shape Poems* schreiben.

What is the poem by Roger McGough about?

The poem expresses the difference between night and day by saying that the sun cannot fool people because just when everything looks especially colourful it leaves and is replaced by the moon.

In what way does the shape of this poem support its meaning?

The first part seems to have a certain regular pattern. This regularity is dissolved from line 10 on where the writing reflects the beginning of the night where all these "golden" things can no longer be seen. At the end of the poem the word "MOON" is written like a notice and thus reflects the lonely appearance of the moon in the sky at night. From line six there are spaces between the first word of each line and the subsequent description of what can be seen during the daytime.

● Use the outline of your school building or a blackboard or anything else that you find typical of your school and make a pencil drawing of it. Now write a sentence or phrase and fill this space with words or trace the outline with words.

● Write a "pyramid" poem by starting with the word "school". In the next line find two words, in the third line three and so on. You may stop at any number of lines. Having reached the bottom of your pyramid, you could also go back to one word by subtracting a word in each further line.

SCHOOL

Many students

_____

_____

_____

_____

_____

_____

_____

● Use the word "school" in the middle of a number of sentences and then write these sentences out. Leave a space between the beginning of the sentence, the word "school" and the end of the sentence. Maybe you can give your poem a certain shape.

I don't like   **school**   on hot days

● Write a poem by using the letters of the word "school" as the beginning of each line.

S _____

C _____

H _____

O _____

O _____

L _____

Roger McGough, *poem about the sun slinking off and pinning up a notice*

the sun

hasn't got me fooled

not for a minute

just when

you're beginning to believe

that   grass is green

and   skies are blue

and   colour is king

hey   ding a ding ding

and

      a

          host

              of

                other

                   golden

                      etceteras

before you know where you are

he's slunk off somewhere   **slink off** go away secretly

and pinned up a notice saying

MOON

Nach dem Lesen dieses Gedichtes stellt man den Schülerinnen und Schülern nun ein weiteres Beispiel für *Shape Poetry* (auch *Concrete Poetry* genannt) vor, das auf plastische Weise zeigt, was mit dem Begriff gemeint sein kann. Die Druckweise von *Forsythia* reflektiert das Aussehen eines Forsythienbusches. Es erfordert einige Aufmerksamkeit zu erkennen, dass weitere Wörter in dem Busch versteckt sind. Diese Wörter sollen von der Klasse entdeckt und gedeutet werden.

Look at the poem *Forsythia* by Mary Ellen Solt. Why is this poem referred to as a shape poem?

This poem is a shape poem because the way it is printed looks like a drawing of a forsythia bush. The letters represent the twigs and leaves of the bush.

Can you make out the words that are written in the Forsythia? What do they mean?

The words are: Forsythia – out – race – spring's – yellow – telegram – hope – insists – action
These words convey the message that forsythias are the very first plants that bloom in spring time. They "outrace" spring, telling people it is near, with their yellow leaves, which are called telegram. The hope that spring will be there soon calls for action.

Having read these poems try to write a shape poem. On your worksheet you have produced a very simple version of a shape poem, now try to be more experimental.

Bei dieser Aufgabe sollte man die Schülerinnen und Schüler nicht thematisch einengen, da sie sehr anspruchsvoll ist. Dennoch werden sicher einige schöne Ergebnisse erzielt werden.

Als Nächstes kann man sich der unterhaltsamen Form der Limericks zuwenden. Zunächst wird wiederum eine Kopiervorlage (mit Limericks) verteilt, damit die Schülerinnen und Schüler das typische Reimschema und metrische Muster in einer Partnerarbeit herausarbeiten können. Danach sind sie aufgefordert, selber solche Fünfzeiler zu verfassen. Es wird leicht erkannt werden, dass der Limerick ein nicht ganz ernst gemeintes Gedicht ist, sondern zur Unterhaltung dient. Dieses Prinzip spricht den Kurs sicher an. Der Impuls, Klassenkameraden oder Lehrer zum Thema eines Limericks zu machen, wird in der Regel gerne aufgenommen und führt zu unterhaltsamen Vorträgen der selbst geschriebenen Texte. Bei Grundkursen kann man anbieten, zunächst einmal einen Limerick auf Deutsch zu verfassen und sich erst dann an die sprachlich schwierige Aufgabe des Verfassens auf Englisch zu machen.

Let us read the limericks. What do you think is the purpose of a limerick?

It seems that limericks deal with people. They are meant to be entertaining and make fun of people.

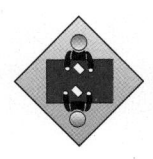

What can you say about the rhyme scheme and metrical pattern of the limerick?

The limerick consists of five lines rhyming: a, a, b, b, a. Its metrical pattern is predominantly iambic with numerous anapests interspersed to heighten its pace.

Mary Ellen Solt, *Forsythia*

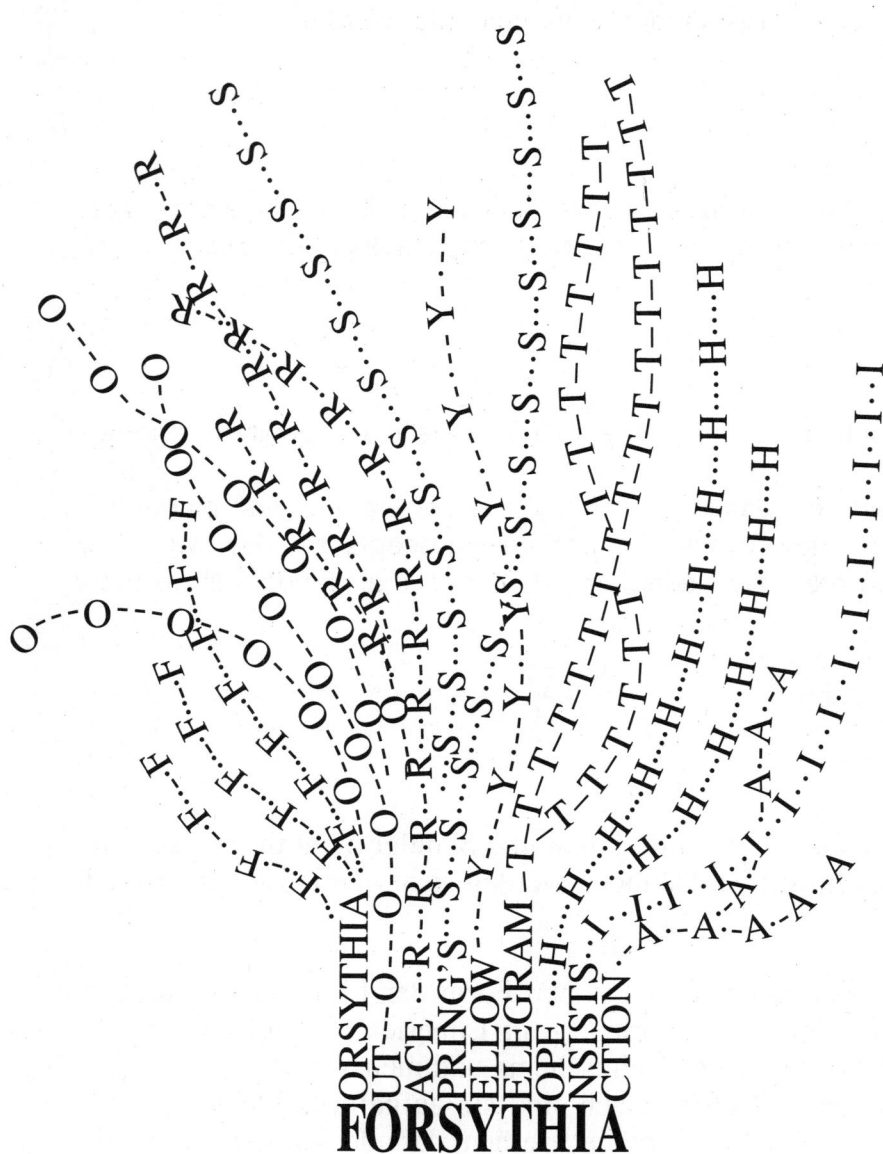

© Schöningh Verlag, Best.-Nr. 041227-4

Limericks

The limerick is furtive and mean;
You must keep her in close quarantine,
    Or she sneaks to the slums
    And promptly becomes
Disorderly, drunk and obscene
(Morris Bishop)

Said Wilbur Wright "Oh, this is grand,
But, Orville, you must understand.
    We've discovered all right
    The secret of flight –
The question is, how do we land?"
(Frank Richards)

There was a young lady of Riga,
Who smiled as she rode on a tiger:
    They returned from the ride
    With the lady inside,
And the smile on the face of the tiger.
(Cosmo Monkhouse)

There was a young fellow called Hall,
Who fell in the spring in the fall;
    'Twould have been sad thing,
    Had he died in the spring,
But he didn't, he died in the fall.
(Anon.)

A jolly young fellow from Yuma
Told an elephant joke to a puma;
    Now his skeleton lies
    Beneath hot western skies –
The puma had no sense of huma.
(Ogden Nash)

© Schöningh Verlag, Best.-Nr. 041227-4

Nach dieser unterhaltsamen Übung werden nun zwei berühmte japanische Formen der Dichtung vorgestellt. Es handelt sich um das Haiku und das Tanka. Bei diesen Formen der Dichtung geht es nicht um Reimschemata und metrische Füße, sondern um die Anzahl der Silben pro Zeile. Inhaltlich handelt es sich nicht um witzige Gedichte, sondern eher um nachdenkliche Texte, die Stimmungen oder Gefühle auf engstem Raum einfangen. Diese Kurzgedichte können von den Schülerinnen und Schülern relativ leicht nachgestaltet werden, da sie ohne jede Reimvorgabe arbeiten können.

Zunächst werden die Beispiele gelesen und Aussagen darüber gemacht, inwiefern sie sich von den Limericks unterscheiden.

In which way do these poems differ from the limericks that we read before?

These poems do not have a set rhyme scheme or metrical pattern. They have to consist of a certain number of syllables per line. Their content is also different from the content of the limericks. Whereas the limericks dealt with people and were funny the haikus and tanka are more serious; they try to capture a certain mood or emotion. In that sense they are more poetic than the limericks.

Nun kann der Kurs aufgefordert werden, selbst ein Haiku oder Tanka zu schreiben. Auch bei dieser Aufgabe werden oft erstaunliche Ergebnisse erzielt.

Now try to write a haiku or tanka. Try to capture a mood, emotion or scene or describe a person.

Je nach „Produktion" können die Schülerergebnisse als kleines Heft für die Schulöffentlichkeit gesammelt, als Beiträge in der Schülerzeitung veröffentlicht oder ins Internet gestellt werden. Falls man diese Einheit in einem 13. Jahrgang durchgeführt hat, bietet sich auch an, einige der von Schülerinnen und Schülern verfassten Gedichte in der Abiturzeitung mit zu veröffentlichen. Auf jeden Fall sollten einige Texte an der Klassenzimmerwand aufgehängt werden und somit einen gewissen Grad an Öffentlichkeit bekommen.

Weitere kreative Aufgaben ergeben sich zuweilen aus Unterrichtsgesprächen und bei der Lektüre der hier vorgestellten Gedichte. Wenn die Schülerinnen und Schüler aufgefordert werden, eigene Gedichte zu verfassen und vorzutragen, werden oft erstaunliche Ergebnisse erzielt. Wichtig ist jedoch in jedem Fall, dass die Schülerinnen und Schüler nicht gezwungen werden, eigene Texte vorzutragen, sondern dass dies immer eine freiwillige Aufgabe ist. In Schülerzeitungen lassen sich Arbeiten ebenso veröffentlichen wie an der Klassenzimmerwand.

Notizen:

_____

_____

_____

_____

_____

Haiku and Tanka

A **haiku**, in its pure form, consists of 17 syllables comprising three lines of 5, 7 and 5 syllables respectively. A haiku is meant to communicate a single idea, image or feeling. Here are some examples:

> Hardly spring, with ice
> still upon the rocks, and yet
> the kisses are bitter.
> (Chiyo)

> *Loneliness*
> A flitting firefly
> "Look! Look there! I start to call –
> But there's no one by.
> (Taigi)

> *City people*
> Townsfolk, it is plain
> carrying red maple leaves
> in the homebound train.
> (Meisetsu)

> In the amber dusk
> Each island dreams its own night.
> The sea swarms with gold.
> (James Kirkup)

Another poem similar to Haiku is **Tanka**; this is a poem consisting of 31 syllables in lines of 5, 7, 5, 7 and 7 syllables. Here is an example by Princess Shikishi, translated by Donald Keene:

> The blossoms have fallen.
> I stare blankly at the world
> Bereft of colour:
> In the wide vacant sky
> The spring rains are falling.

Textnachweise

- **Don Shiach, *Prose and Poetry*, Cambridge University Press 1996**
  Chiyo, Taigi, Meisetsu, James Kirkup (Haikus) (p. 148)
- **Peter Abbs and John Richardson, *The Forms of Poetry*, Cambridge University Press 1990**
  Zulfiker Ghose, *Geography Lesson* (p. 47)
  D. H. Lawrence, *To Women, As Far As I Am Concerned* (p. 137)
  Gavin Ewart, *Ending* (p. 172)
  Rupert Brooke, *Sonnet* (p. 202)
- **Roy J. Cook, *One hundred and One Famous Poems*, Barnes & Noble, New York 1993**
  William Wordsworth, *The Daffodils* (p. 16)
  George Washington Doane, *Life Sculpture* (p. 146)
  John Keats, *Ode to a Grecian Urn* (p. 150)
  William Shakespeare, *Sonnet 73* (p. 85)
- **Pat McLoughlin, *Woman's Hour 50th Anniversary Poetry Collection*, Penguin 1996**
  Sheila Perry, *In the Beginning was the Word* (p. 26)
  Lois Clark, *Picture from the Blitz* (p. 50)
  Lynn Peters, *Why Dorothy Wordsworth is not as famous as her Brother* (p. 108)
- **Adrian Barlow, *The Calling of Kindred*, Poems from the English-speaking world, Cambridge University Press 1993**
  William Blake, *The Tiger* (p. 81)
- **Jon Stallworthy, *The Oxford Book of War Poetry*, Oxford University Press 1984**
  Peter Porter, *Your Attention, Please* (p. 338); © Peter Porter
- **Geoffrey Moore, *The Penguin Book of American Verse*, Penguin 1977**
  William Carlos Williams, *This is Just to Say* (p. 265) *The Red Wheelbarrow* (p. 264)
- **Pat Ingoldsby, *See Liz, She Spins*, Willow Publications, Dublin, 1997**
  Open Season (p. 88)
- ***The Norton Anthology of English Literature*, Volume I, New York 1979**
  Andrew Marwell, *To His Coy Mistress* (p. 1361)
  John Milton, *Sonnet VII* (p. 1395)
- ***The Complete Works of Oscar Wilde*, Book Club Associates, London 1980**
  Oscar Wilde, *The Ballad of Reading Goal* (p. 843)
- ***Paths into Poetry*, Joanne Collie and Gillian Porter Ladousse, Oxford University Press, 1991**
  Roger McGough, *poem about the sun slinking off and pinning up a notice*; © Jonathan Cape Publishers
- ***The Penguin Book of Limericks*, E. O. Parrott, London 1983**
  Morris Bishop (p. 21)
  Frank Richards (p. 79)
  Cosmo Monkhouse (p. 106)
  Anon. (p. 108)
  Ogden Nash (p. 108)
- Derek Walcott, *A Country Club Romance:* © Farrar, Straus & Giroux, New York
- Seamus Heaney, *Death of a Naturalist,* from: S. Heaney, *Death of a Naturalist,* © Faber and Faber Ltd., London

- **W. H. Auden, *Collected Poems,* Faber and Faber Ltd., London**
  W. H. Auden, *Victor*
- Jeni Couzyn, *Complaint of the Water:* © Andrew Mann Ltd., London
- ***Men Who March Away,* Poems of the First World War, I.M. Parsons, Chatto & Windus, London 1965**
  Herbert Asquith, *The Volunteer* (p. 41)
  Siegfried Sassoon, *The General* (p. 75)
- **Adrian Henri et al., *The Mersey Sound,* Penguin, Harmondsworth 1983**
  Adrian Henri, *The New, Fast, Automatic Daffodils* (p. 49)
- Byrne/Frantz/Weymouth/Harrison/Jock, *(Nothing but) Flowers:* © International Music Publications and Warner Chappell Music, Essex
- **Donald Keene (ed.), *Anthology of Japanese Literature,* Grove Press Inc., New York 1985**
  Princess Shikishi, *Tanka* (translated by Donald Keene)
- ***A Book of Women Poets,* ed. Barnstow A & W, Schocken Books, New York**
  Mary Ellen Solt, *Forsythia* (from: Mary Ellen Solt, *Flowers in Concrete*)
- *Grass* from CHICAGO POEMS by Carl Sandburg, copyright 1916 by Holt, Rinehart and Winston and renewed 1944 by Carl Sandburg, reprinted by permission of Harcourt, Inc.

Unterrichtsmodelle und Textausgaben

NEU

EINFACH ENGLISCH

Edited by Hans Kröger

J. B. Priestley
An Inspector Calls
by Hans Kröger
Textausgabe. 80 S. kart., Best.-Nr. 041200 0
Unterrichtsmodell. 64 S. DIN A4, kart.,
Best.-Nr. 041201 0

T. C. Boyle
The Tortilla Curtain
by Wiltrud Frenken, Angela Luz and Brigitte Prischtt
Unterrichtsmodell. 75 S. DIN A4, kart.,
Best.-Nr. 041203 7

Charles Webb
The Graduate
by Louise Nübold
Unterrichtsmodell. 60 S. DIN A4, kart.,
Best.-Nr. 041205 3

Arthur Miller
The Crucible
by Hans-Christoph Ramm
Unterrichtsmodell. 84 S. DIN A4, kart.,
Best.-Nr. 041209 6

Monty Python
by Engelbert Thaler
Unterrichtsmodell. 71 S. DIN A4, kart.,
Best.-Nr. 041221 5

William Golding
Lord of the Flies
by Angela Luz, Brigitte Prischtt and Wiltrud Frenken
Unterrichtsmodell. 98 S. DIN A4, kart.,
Best.-Nr. 041217 7

Mark Behr
The Smell of Apples
by Anno Ortmeier
Unterrichtsmodell. 77 S. DIN A4, kart.,
Best.-Nr. 041215 0

American Beauty
by Wiltrud Frenken, Brigitte Prischtt and Angela Luz
Unterrichtsmodell. 87 S. DIN A4, kart.,
Best.-Nr. 041225 8

Criminals & Detectives
by Christine Hoidis-Fehler
Textausgabe. 98 S., kart., Best.-Nr. 041206 1
Unterrichtsmodell. 96 S. DIN A4, kart., Best.-Nr. 041207 X

Forrest Gump
by Kornelius Nelles and Karsten Witsch
Unterrichtsmodell. 65 S. DIN A4, kart.,
Best.-Nr. 041231 2

Dead Poets Society
by Engelbert Thaler
Unterrichtsmodell. 67 S. DIN A4, kart.,
Best.-Nr. 041255 x

Roman Polanski
Macbeth
by Antje Blume
Unterrichtsmodell. 103 S. DIN A4, kart.,
Best.-Nr. 041235 5

In Vorbereitung:

Thunderheart
by Wiltrud Frenken, Angela Luz and Brigitte Prischtt
Unterrichtsmodell. ca. 80 S. DIN A4, kart.,
Best.-Nr. 041211 6

B. MacLaverty
Cal
by Jürgen Velsinger
Unterrichtsmodell. ca. 64 S. DIN A4, kart.,
Best.-Nr. 041239 8

Aldous Huxley
Brave New World
by Wiltrud Frenken, Angela Luz and Brigitte Prischtt
Unterrichtsmodell. ca. 80 S. DIN A4, kart.,
Best.-Nr. 041249 5 ·

Fordern Sie unseren Prospekt zur Reihe an:
Informationen zum Nulltarif ✆ 08 00 / 1 81 87 87

SCHÖNINGH VERLAG
im Westermann Schulbuchverlag GmbH
Postfach 2540 · 33055 Paderborn

Schöningh

E-Mail: info@schoeningh.de
Internet: http://www.schoeningh.de